Reader Praise for *We H*

D1239349

"Once in a great while, there comes ... ... pow-erfully, and humanely to a crucial issue of the time. *We Have All Been the 'Others'* is that book for our time. A relatable memoir that vividly recounts what it was like to grow up as an Italian immigrant family in Chicago and a compelling, clear-eyed reflection on racial division in America, this book both holds up a mirror to what is unlovely and hateful in our common history, and helps us simultaneously to see and fashion a redemptive path. Deeply researched, laced with humor, propelled by winsome narrative, this daughter's nuanced tribute to her larger-than-life father compels us to remember the commonalities, both good and bad, that bind us as families, communities, and citizens. And at a time when our country appears relentlessly polarized, *We Have All Been the 'Others'* regenerates hope and offers practical pathways for empathetic living in a diverse world."

—GLYNDA A. HULL, ELIZABETH H. and EUGENE A. SHURTLEFF CHAIR; Faculty Director, Undergraduate Studies, and Center for Teaching and Learning School of Education, University of California, Berkeley

"Poignant, thought-provoking, and delightful!"

—Valerie Miles, DMin, PhD; Professor, Ministerial Leadership & Practical Theology, Graduate Theological Union; Core Doctoral Faculty, Religion & Practice Department, Theology & Ethics Department

"Wow! Loved this book. I am so impressed by the depth and vision reflected in the author's massive research and compassionate writing. Once I started reading, I was so caught up in the narrative that I have to admit, I couldn't edit it, I had to let go of my 'edit' cap and just read for pure pleasure. Pat did a fabulous job weaving family history within the context of US history—I learned so much—and I think this fundamental 'merger' makes this book unique. The last chapters, suggesting possible solutions and a checklist for readers to pursue their own family history, also add a dimension to the book that you don't often see. The book defies genre but I would place it in a niche of personal memoirs and spiritual reflection—a small, compact book, stuffed with so much information and warm memories that we can all share in the author's love of family. I found the book inspirational and heart-warming, plus the education, and so deserving of publication and widespread distribution." —ANN CURRAN, Writer, Editor

"This is a timely, warm-hearted book rehabilitating the image of immigrants, often disparaged in America and other countries. Marino, a second-generation Italian American and a history buff, pays tribute to her first-generation father, a son of immigrants, enumerating his many valuable life lessons that nurtured her concern for fairness and equal access to the American Dream for everyone. The book is sprinkled with essential historical information and ideas for creating a more just America; as well as vivid, loving stories of Marino's large Italian-American family, some of them immigrants, and their important contributions to this country."

—RALPH DRANOW, editor and poet; author, *A New Life,* co-author with Daniel Marlin, *At Work on the Garments of Refuge*

"This warm-hearted history-as-memoir (or memoir-as-history) brings us from the microcosm—the richly detailed world of Pat's own Italian-American upbringing in Chicago—into the macrocosm of life in the United States at this time, addressing its fault lines, its compromised vision, and its promise towards renewal: a New American Dream. In reading Pat's richly detailed narrative, I came away with a sharpened understanding of the lives of my own immigrant relatives, and a deepened compassion for other groups of people here from many other shores. The "lessons" that Pat learned from her police-detective father, Alexander Francis Marino, which have helped her to navigate life in America and make it a better place, provide a springboard for readers to explore their own comparable heritage of wisdom, and join her in envisioning and contributing to a new American Dream."

—NAOMI ROSE, author, *Starting Your Book: A Guide to Navigating the Blank Page by Listening to What's Inside You,* and *MotherWealth: The Feminine Path to Money*

WE HAVE ALL BEEN
THE "OTHERS"

Reflections of a First-Generation's Daughter
on Belonging, Democracy, and a
New American Dream

Patricia J. Marino

Rose Press
Oakland, California

Rose Press
www.rosepress.com
rosepressbooks@yahoo.com
Naomi Rose, Publisher

Note: Some names of persons mentioned in the book have been changed to protect the feelings of their descendants. Otherwise, the actual names and affiliations have been used.

Cover illustration and interior illustrations:
Elena Karoumpali, L1graphics /
https://99designs.com/profiles/l1graphics

Developmental Editing / Copyediting / Graphics Coordinator:
Naomi Rose / *www.naomirose.net*

Proofreading:
Gabriel Steinfeld / *www.gabrielsteinfeld.com*

Book Design and Typesetting:
Margaret Copeland, Terragrafix / *www.terragrafix.com*

Printed in the United States of America

First printing 2023

ISBN# 978-0-9816278-9-2

To Alex, the teacher of my youth in many ways,
and to my late, dear, and greatly missed husband, Al,
who supported me in who I became—
both strong men in my life,
both who gave love as the yeast for growth.

Contents

Preface ix

Lessons I Learned from My Father xii

Introduction 1

PART I: Remembering Family, and Our Place in the American Dream 5

Chapter 1: Remembering Fairfield Avenue 7

Chapter 2: The Reckoning 19

Chapter 3: The Setting of the Joy: Lessons from the Alexander
Francis School of Life 29

Lesson #1: Laws Don't Always Equal Right / A Portrait of
Dirty Harry 36

Lesson #2: Call Out Hypocrisy / Alex and Sinatra 42

Lesson #3: Mixing with the Mob is a Death Knell / Alex and
Sinatra. 44

Lesson #4: Strive to Learn Toughness through Adversity /
Alex and Working the System 48

Lesson #5: Keep Your Commitments / Alex and LBJ. 52

Chapter 4: 902 Cambridge Avenue—The Old Neighborhood. 59

Lesson #6: Bring Fairness to the Problem—Equality Is the Gold
Standard / Alex the Detective 67

Lesson #7: See the Human in the Stereotype / Alex and World War
II, at Home and Abroad 74

Lesson #8 – Love as the Yeast for Growth—Can Food and Love
Bridge Assimilation? / Alex's Family DNA 77

Chapter 5: The Part of Our Part. 85

Lesson #9: The "Other" Is YOU / Those Who Came Before 85

Chapter 6: Pragmatism and the Power Structure. 97

Lesson #10: Speak Truth to Power / Alex and the Church. 97

Example 1—Excommunication-Gate 99

Example 2—The Green Stamp Caper 101

PART II: Understanding Our Collective History to See Us All as
Americans. 109

Chapter 7: My Suffering, My Rights, My Governance 111

Chapter 8: The Sacred Trust—Promises Unfulfilled 121

Lesson #11: Face Your Fears and Your Truth / Our Collective
Immigrant Experience 121

*When Sicilians Were Considered "Too Black" for the South and
Even the North* 122
The Earliest Americans and Their Struggles for Full Inclusion. . . 128
The "Assimilation" of Native Americans and African Americans 131
The Fear of "Different". 137
A Narcissistic Spin on the American Dream 139
Course-Correcting the American Dream 139

Chapter 9: Fragments to Fulfillment: Lesson #7 Revisited—See the
Human in the Stereotype—or Who Gets to Have Access to Rights? . 143
Capitalism with a Conscience 150
Thinking Big—Recommendations on Balancing the Scale 153
*Tears to Cheers 155 / Reparations 156 / Education Re-Thought
158 / Instigate a Massive Communication Strategy 161 / Political
Non-Partisanship 162 / Economic Infusions 163/ New Ways to
Think About Policing 165*
Some Afterthoughts. 167
Where Are We In Our Country? A Gut Check 169

Chapter 10: Beloved Community—A Nostalgia for Community . . . 171
And Some Not-So-Nostalgic Aspects. 174
My Family's Own Beloved Community. 179

Chapter 11: Lessons from America—Reflections on Adding Your
Pieces to the American Mosaic 185
Reflections on Your Family 186
Reflections on Re-Thinking the American Dream 186
Reflections on the Vision of a New American Dream 187

Epilogue: Lessons Learned in the Alexander Francis School of Life
and Their Translation to a Re-Imagined American Dream 191

To Continue the Conversation... 197
Endnotes. 199
Photos & Illustrations. 204
Acknowledgments. 206
About the Author 209
About Rose Press 210

Preface

As a continuous student of history wanting to look deeper into my own roots, I began to see aspects of American history that were related to my family's experience on a larger scale. I value history's ability to provide a blueprint for understanding present dilemmas, as well as areas of agreement that can help us construct a roadmap to living well in the future—if we listen to the lessons of the past.

What began as a memoir of my father and the lessons he taught me morphed into a reflection on immigration, assimilation, and what it means to be an American. Those lessons provided a lens on the faults and fissures at play today in American society and what they might teach us as to how to bridge the political and social divide.

As a history teacher in the 1970s, I concluded that many people don't really have a broad knowledge of U.S. history or have only one perspective on it. There are aspects of U.S. history that either have not been included or have been written from the perception of the victor. Fifty years ago, when I was teaching high school juniors and seniors, primarily African American and Hispanic, there was a dearth of information about slavery or the contributions of former enslaved peoples or Native Americans and other non-white members of our American community. To fill in the gap, I incorporated into our lessons books such as *Bury My Heart at Wounded Knee*, *Black Elk Speaks*, and *Custer Died for Your Sins*. I also made sure to include information on people like Benjamin Bannecker, the inventor; Sojourner Truth, the poet; James Armistead, the American spy; and Black Hawk, the Native American who stood his ground in Illinois, during what came to be called the Black Hawk War. These were all people who had suffered from ill treatment in our country, but gave back to America from the beginning.

This lack of incorporating key historical events to do with African Americans, Native Americans, and other people of color has had some bearing on the stereotyping of various groups of people, and worse. One of my reasons for assigning my students these kinds of books was to open them up to the actual *experiences* of African Americans, Hispanics, and Native Americans, so the students could see them as human beings, as contributors. My students began to have a pride in themselves and who their ancestors were.

As that former history teacher so long ago, and as a continuous student of history, I wanted to look deeper into my own roots. In taking that closer look, I began to see aspects of American history that were related to my family's experience on a larger scale. I value history's ability to provide a blueprint for understanding present dilemmas, as well as areas of agreement that can help us construct a roadmap to living well in the future—*if* we listen to the lessons of the past.

This book is a walk through my family history, but perhaps there are elements that will reflect your own history. I have included a call to action in the latter part of the book, because I think we all have a role to play in healing the great divide and getting back to who we really are—Americans! not Republicans, Democrats, red, black, yellow, white, or brown. First and foremost, we are human beings who happen to take residence in and feel a belonging to the ideal of America.

A note on some of the factual aspects of this book: The historical reports are factual to the best of my knowledge, but the personal details, stories and conversations relayed in this book come from my remembrances, either real or imagined. In speaking with my brother, who is older than I am, I discovered that he does not recall some of the anecdotes that, for some reason, have stuck in my brain. I have written dialogues—for example, of conversations that my mother would have had with my father, or that would have occurred between my father and his brother. The words are not exact, but I wrote them as those people *would* have said them, or with the tone to capture what *would have been* the tenor of a conversation—all to illustrate or bring dimensionality to the people populating these pages.

I have also changed the names, in some instances, to protect any descendants of people from long ago who might take umbrage with my characterization of their relative. In other cases, I have used the actual names, since it's simply a matter of listing who was in my neighborhood at the time. Yet whether designated as themselves or in compassionate disguise, the characters named in this memoir are real and an essential part of the fabric that made up Arcadia Terrace—at least my part of Arcadia Terrace—in Chicago, where I grew up in the 1950s and '60s.

Lessons I Learned from My Father

Here are the major lessons that I learned from my father, Alexander Francis Marino, which influenced my writing about Belonging, Democracy, and a New American Dream. They are explored in more detail in the chapters of this book.

LESSON #1: Laws Don't Always Equal Right

Some laws are good, some—not so much. Laws do not always mean right. (*See* Chapter 3)

LESSON #2: Call Out Hypocrisy

Call out hypocrisy even when it is difficult or may cost you something of value, whether tangible or intangible. The price for not addressing hypocrisy can be a heavier one than losing the valued thing. (*See* Chapter 3)

LESSON #3: Mixing With the Mob Is a Death Knell

Mixing with the mob could mean you might wear some rather heavy shoes in water—not a good combination. While this is a literal lesson that might not apply to all people and circumstances, an extension of this concept is learning to make good choices, including choosing the company you keep. (*See* Chapter 3)

LESSON #4: Strive to Learn Toughness Through Adversity

I gained toughness from watching my father get knocked down by life and get back up despite adversity. (*See* Chapter 3)

LESSON 5: Keep Your Commitments

For my Dad, keeping your commitments was "the handshake," the personal promise that you would deliver on what you said. Not doing so would be a dishonor, a signal that you could not be trusted. Alex learned on his police-force days that trust in your partner was at the heart of staying alive, and trust was and is at the core of commitments. (*See* Chapter 3)

LESSON 6: Bring Fairness to the Problem—Equality Is the Gold Standard

"Lady Law" should be equal for everyone, not just those whom we favor, or who can do us favors, or who can get us out of trouble. This is still a work in progress. (*See* Chapter 4)

LESSON 7: See the Human in the Stereotype . . .

...so that we are not imprisoned by our generalizations—and so that the real people, who collectively make up a given general category, aren't imprisoned in boxes of narrow perspectives. (*See* Chapter 4)

LESSON 8: Love as the Yeast for Growth—Can Food and Love Bridge Assimilation?

Love is indeed the yeast for growth. While one can succeed without it, I suppose, still the love of family, friends, and community provides the strength to move forward. (*See* Chapter 4)

LESSON #9: The "Other" Is You

The Other is *indeed* you. A lesson indirectly taught by Alexander Francis was not to forget that once upon a time, *you* were "the other"—that my grandparents Peter and Maria were the "other," not so welcomed by those already here. (*See* Chapter 5)

LESSON #10: Speak Truth to Power

Power doesn't always equate to right, to problem solving, or to getting anything done. As The Field Golf Incident with Monsignor H. wasn't corrupt in the sense of anything visible, or with landmark repercussions; but it taught me to question power, to question when something doesn't seem quite right. It was a lesson in understanding consequences, both short-term and long-term. (*See* Chapter 6)

LESSON #11: Face Your Fears and Your Truth

This is about remembering where we have all come from; that each of our families' ancestors were at one time or other considered *"the other,"* the not-so-welcomed. (*See* Chapter 8)

Introduction

It is the pieces of so many different cultures—so many differ-
ent expectations, hopes, and dreams—that, over centuries, have
been linked together in a changing mosaic to reflect the growing
depth of stories, past, present, and future. Each piece, while dif-
ferent, aligns with the other pieces to begin to make a whole,
a fuller portrait. The mosaic, so painstakingly crafted, is still a
work in progress.

When I started this work, it was to capture the essence of my Dad, Alexander Francis Marino, and the great big Italian family I was born into and who raised me. I related to the film, *My Big Fat Greek Wedding*. Like the Greeks, Italians had the habit of using the same given names throughout the extended family. Case in point: there were three sons, two of my two uncles, all my male cousins, and my brother—all with the same name. There was Uncle Larry's "Peter," Uncle Nick's "Peter," and—in our immediate family—Alex's "Peter"; so when we were at the larger family gatherings and someone shouted out, "Pete," all three Peters would turn around. You had to qualify *which* Pete by saying "Uncle Larry's Pete" or in some other form the "appropriate" Pete. Just change the Greek background and food in the movie for Italian, and a lot of that was our family, although not as ethno-centric. I grew up in the 1950s and '60s in a European-diverse neighborhood with Irish, Italian, Polish, Czech, and other East European nationalities, Jews, Catholics, Protestants, and who knows whom else.

As the writing evolved, however, it took on a life of its own. In looking back on my Dad's life as a first-generation son of Italian immigrants born in the early 1900s, I wondered how his life and that of his family added to the mosaic of American life. I wondered about all those immigrants, those brought here by force, by debt (as with indentured servants), and by conscious or unconscious decisions for a better life in pursuit of that American dream. According to the Webster dictionary, the American Dream is "a happy way of living that is thought of by many Americans as something that can be achieved by anyone in the U.S., especially by working hard and becoming successful."[1] Or as stated in the article, "What is the American Dream?" by Amadeo and Catalano, "The American dream is the idea that every U.S. citizen and documented immigrant is bestowed with the equal opportunity to achieve upward mobility and success."[2] And while this has often meant having a good job, a house, and giving a good education to one's children, it is an ever-evolving concept that I think will change to encompass the thoughts, cultures, and beliefs of those still waiting to add their own design to the mosaic of American life. Thinking about my own grandparents whom I never knew and my surrogate *nonna* and *nonno*, Aunt Grace and Uncle Vito, I wondered about their assimilation and how that contrasted with those of two groups of Americans—Native Americans and African Americans—whose "upward mobility and success" has had its share of roadblocks in our history.

It is the pieces of so many different cultures—so many different expectations, hopes, and dreams—that, over centuries, have been linked together in a changing mosaic to reflect the growing depth of stories, past, present, and future. Each piece, while different, aligns with the other pieces to begin to make a whole, a fuller portrait. This whole was encapsulated in the concepts crafted by the Founding Fathers, steeped in ancient Greek and Roman philosophy, and hewed over centuries by thoughts and actions from the Magna Carta to Rousseau's "noble savage" and more. Concepts crafted by flawed men—many of whom were slaveholders themselves, men who did not recognize women's rights (except good ol' Ben Franklin) or those of anyone not white. But nevertheless, what they envisioned set in motion that ability for my grandparents and their offspring, Alexander Francis and his nine brothers and sisters, to find a home, a place to become part of that American dream. To become more American than Italian.

The mosaic, so painstakingly crafted, is still a work in progress. While it tells a unique and unfolding story, there are missing pieces that make it less than whole, less of a story than what it could be. While Italians faced discrimination as immigrants, chastised for their perceived "lack of intelligence"—and for those from Southern Italy, like Aunt Grace and Uncle Vito, who were darker-skinned—within a short time frame, many became homeowners and business owners. I wondered why my Dad, my Uncle Larry, and my Grandfather Peter were absorbed into America faster than those who have been here the longest—the Native American and African American, whose American dream, upward mobility, and success, it seems to me, are still only partially realized. Their pieces of the mosaic are waiting to be added, in the fullest sense.

My own journey back to that neighborhood in Chicago, to a time and place of the 1950s and '60s—to that Irish, Jewish, Polish, Lithuanian, Mexican, and more place to understand the many lessons my Dad taught me—also took me on a journey of immigration and how the separate becomes the whole. Dad taught me many lessons that he unknowingly passed along; and—like the Founding Fathers—he was, as I am, as we all are, flawed. It is in striving for "our better angels" that we do indeed add our own mosaic of food, culture, and ways of being from distant lands and times to create a portrait of an America that reflects the diversity and the promise of this young nation.

I find it interesting that the U.S. Mint used the words, *e pluribus unum* in 1795, "out of many, one"—probably emphasizing the unity of 13 former and disparate colonies. I do believe that ignorance of our own history—of some parts of that history that have been suppressed, distorted, or not telling the whole story—plays a part in formerly enslaved people, African Americans and Native Americans, not taking their seats equally at this American table. I remember some neighborhood stories about how other ethnic groups viewed my Uncle Vito or Aunt Grace as perhaps not "American enough," and I don't recall reading anything about Italian immigration in my U.S. history courses in high school, other than there were many who emigrated, or something about Columbus.

Much of Native American and African American history is missing from high school courses even now. In my day, it was almost non-existent; or, if covered, there was a definite rewrite to make slavery or the land-grab of the 19th century (that theory of Manifest Destiny) more palatable. Understanding our history and facing its truth enables the mosaic to continue to shape. My memories of Aunt Grace and Uncle Vito, with their broken English and their Sicilian love of cooking, growing vegetables, music, "basaball," and family taught me that we all come from some other place (either recently or in the distant past), and somehow our families became Americans. We were all once the "others."

This book is about lessons learned—not just for me in my family, but also for all of us: the lessons of immigration, the lessons of failure, success, and inclusion.

There is more work to be done specifically for and with the missing pieces. Just as mosaic pieces by themselves are only fragments of a picture, mosaics pieced together form a whole that tells a better story and of *what could be*!

Here is my story....

PART I

Remembering Family, and Our Place in the American Dream

CHAPTER 1

Remembering Fairfield Avenue

I was surrounded by characters, every single one of whom I still remember and love. These were the first "builders" of my character, of the person whom I have become. Each had their unique character, their own way of approaching life. I always carry with me the lessons I learned from them. But most especially, I carry the life lessons from my Dad, even though in my teenage and college years I wasn't as close to him as to my Mom. But looking back, it was my Dad's lessons that I have taken with me on my own journey.

think often of my family and growing up in Chicago in the 1950s and '60s. At that time, I almost felt "suffocated" by the communal life in my family—my immediate family upstairs, and my aunts, uncles, and older cousin "Honey" downstairs; by the parade of relations and friends who streamed in and out of our two-flat weekly and often daily; by my neighborhood, where everyone knew almost everyone. My Dad, Alexander Francis, the patriarch of the Fairfield Avenue crew, was an interesting mix of volatility, gregariousness, warmth, overwhelmingness and style. You always knew when he was in the room. My Mom was no shrinking violet, either; she had a depth to her that I caught glimpses of, a strength of character that welcomed the world with laughter and humor despite an early childhood marked with some grief. From the time I was a girl, I wanted to see the world, a poignant wish that my Mom often talked about for herself. She wanted to be a great adventuress like Jack London's wife. She actually told me that one day, when she was visiting Oakland, California (Jack London's

Mom and Dad
(Ann Bublis Marino and
Alexander Francis Marino)

stomping grounds), where I had moved after marrying and where I still live now.

My "suffocation" factor was that of youth, wanting to try my wings. That feeling, however, was superseded by the warmth and love I knew resided in that home on Fairfield Avenue. I was surrounded by characters, every single one of whom I still remember and love. As I was preparing to leave Chicago in June of 1974 to go with my husband to return to his hometown of Oakland, I went to say my good-byes to my Uncle Vito and Aunt Grace.

I remember Vito sitting at his kitchen table, tears welling up in his eyes. He took my hands in his rough-hewn rounded paws, aged and scored by years of working, driving railroad spikes, and paving streets—this old Sicilian ancestral farmer who said, "Pally Jo [because that was how *I* would pronounce Pattie Jo when I was little], I'll never see you again; I love you." I never did see him again. He died about one year later. How I miss him to this day—this squat, stocky, gruff, 5' by 5' Italian immigrant who was my surrogate grandfather (my real *nonno* had died long before); this Fiorello La Guardia character who smoked stogy black Cuban cigars, retreated to our basement to watch "basaball" (the Cubs, in particular) to escape all the women in the house; who shouted at the neighborhood kids, when they played or ran across his small patch of grass, "Offa the grass!" from the basement window. He looked fierce, but was really more like the teddy bear "Corduroy" with a big heart. Standing by his side his entire life and raising the Marino brood was Aunt Grace, who was nicknamed "Tonto" because of the bandanas she wore around her head for headaches, whose language was always food, spoken on a regular basis with fried dough after school and holiday extravaganzas. Through the Great Depression and World War II era, Vito and Grace raised a family who contributed to this country we call home.

Living with Grace and Vito were Grace's two sisters—Frances, who never married, and Lena, who married late in life—and Grace's daughter, whom we called "Honey," perennially plagued by illness,

Aunt Grace, Uncle Vito and daughter, Honey

which (we discovered later) was attributable to her bout with rheumatic fever in her childhood. Frances had a sharp mind and an affinity for math. Both she and Lena were "lookers," as people would say in their day—auburn hair, gray-blue eyes, and touches of freckles, all relic DNA from centuries-old Viking and Vandal raids and Norman conquests. Lena was the more outgoing, social and fun-loving; Frances, more reserved. Both went to work for Carson Pirie Scott as buyers for jewelry, cosmetics, and other retail merchandise lines. Lena rose to assistant buyer and made her first big trip to New York, highly unusual for a woman then. My brother Pete and the family drove with her to Midway Airport (no O'Hare, then) to see her off.

The sisters loved to dance, enjoyed music, went to an all-girls Catholic high school, and were heavily chaperoned by their six very dominant brothers—a holdover, I am sure, of their Sicilian village upbringing on Cambridge Avenue in the 1920s and '30s. Part of this was good; but that cautiousness and clinging to some old-world traditions prevented Frances from marrying a divorced man with two children from New York (the story is that my Grandmother Maria would have none of this "divorce" in the family), and my Aunt Lena married

Lena and Frances

late in life—my Uncle Lou, her German-descended ex-boss, who had worked as a buyer for Marshall Field & Company.

Aunt Frances was a good baseball player, playing sand-lot ball with her brothers in the early 1930s, begrudgingly afforded this opportunity only when the team needed a stand-in. I often think what she might have done, given her talent, in another era and with another mindset—women can do amazing things—and I was sad to see her almost devolution into a hermit-like status as her big family began to literally die off over the years. She always had a tendency to OCD, whisking away dishes with the speed of light as you tried to finish your meal with the last morsel heading to your mouth, Frances hovering like a nervous waiter. The OCD only became more egregious as her hermit status took over. However, I also remember the Frances of her earlier days, when I was little, who often would move the dining-room table back closer to the wall after a special birthday or anniversary meal for one of the family, put on music, and get us all dancing and laughing. My love for music, from Cole Porter to Satchmo to Bruno Mars, comes from not only my Dad's poker parties but also these impromptu "dance halls."

Lena had a great sense of fashion and taking care of one's body—not exercise, mind you, but using the right cosmetics, washing up in the evening and using good-quality moisturizers, staying far away from the sun, and remembering, "Pally Jo, your neck is part of your face" (a mantra to always moisturize face, neck, and décolletage!). My German-ancestored-by-marriage Uncle Lou's mandate handed down to me was to stand up straight and shoulders back! Lena was more adventurous, although both aunts accompanied me on trips to Boston and other parts of New England in 1961, with Uncle Lou insisting that we visit Filene's Department Store, a monument as worthy as Faneuil Hall or Beacon Hill. Uncle Lou wanted Lena to move with him to Santa Barbara in the '50s because he had seen California on many business trips to flagship stores in LA and elsewhere. I often wonder how our lives would have changed if that had happened, but Lena was too tied to her siblings to make that crossing. Little did I ever dream that *I* would become a Californian so many years later.

The trail of aunts and uncles that stopped by "the house" (for it seemed like Fairfield was the citadel for the Marino clan) on any given day brought gifts, cookies, wine, cheese, produce, a cacophony of conversations and arguments, strategy sessions, laughter and sadness sometimes, and news of friends' or relatives' illnesses and tragedies. Uncle Larry was the "book-learner" brother, as my Dad so disdainfully

Justinian Society (125 Justinians in DC, 1960s).
Uncle Larry is in second row from back.

Young Uncle Larry

called him. Dad thought Larry didn't have the sense he was born with. Yet Larry would go on to be admitted to the bar of the U.S. Supreme Court as a member of the Justinian Society of Lawyers in 1960. The six brothers were something to behold when they all got together, five of the six being 6 feet tall or more, with long, lean bodies— inherited, I am sure, from Grandpa Marino, with his piercing blue eyes and stature. Only Uncle Jasper, who looks like the diminutive Dr. Fauci, was about 5' 7", maybe shorter.

In the first decade of the 1900s, Larry had been identified early by a public-school principal as very bright and had been encouraged to pursue college—highly unusual, in those days, for a first-generation son of an immigrant. The five other brothers finished high school, several of them attending night school and working during the day to put Larry through college and eventually law school. I often wonder what it must have been like for Uncle Larry, having had the advantage of an expanded horizon through education, but still living in this quasi-Italian village on Cambridge Avenue. Both he and my Dad clashed often, and Larry had the volatile temper that runs through some of the Marinos. As the story goes, Larry was upset back during Prohibition about a job Uncle Pete and Dad had that seemed just fine to the two of them.

"Jesus Christ, Larry, why are you so exercised about Pete and I making some money for the family by bringing some booze to the court judges? They asked for it! We're just accommodating."

"It's against the law," screamed Larry. *"Remember Prohibition: there's not supposed to be any sales, any transactions for liquor in the City. I don't know, sometimes you have your head up your ass!"*

This is an imagined heated argument, but it has the color and verbiage that both men would have used.

I remember talking to Larry, as I grew older—about politics, the family, college, and more. His great gift to me and my brother was his collection of the Harvard Classics, which I still have to this day: words printed in miniscule on sheer, paper-thin pages, but which took me to the worlds of Dickens, Twain, and Cooper's *The Last of the Mohicans*. In fact, my sister has forever carried the nickname of Magua (why, I don't know), which emerged from those pages. I still read poems from Larry's book of poetry, *The Lake English Classics*, published by Scott Foresman in 1928. It actually has my Uncle Pete's very beautiful signature in it, and the address "902 Cambridge Avenue, Chicago, Illinois"—the family's first home when they immigrated to Chicago from Louisiana—so the book must have been passed around. Included were Longfellow, Shakespeare, Tennyson, Milton, Hawthorne, Elliot, and more. Ah, those sneaky Italians reading those English and American writers. These books were my first educators.

Like Grace, Larry had more of that swarthy, darker complexion, and gray-blue eyes reminding me more of East than West. When my Dad passed away many years later, I had to meet with Uncle Larry to sort out my Dad's affairs. I was never so exhausted by trying to keep up with this then-75+-year-old lawyer, with those elongated legs striding Chicago's very long downtown blocks, going from one office to another to do "the sort." Larry believed in a brewer's-yeast concoction, drinking it every morning. His energy level belied his age. And for sure, he reflected some of the Marinos' real or imagined ADD—they were always in constant motion, like protons and neutrons fighting for life in the atom.

Uncle Pete was unbelievably good-looking, not quite as tall as the others but close, with those piercing blue eyes, as if Grandpa Pete were almost looking through him. He was a World War II veteran, having served at the Battle of the Bulge under Patton, the steel plates in his body a constant reminder of that time and place. He was active, fast, quick-witted; he loved to fish and play baseball, and sometimes he let me play in the outfield at the big Italian-American picnics we occasionally attended. My biggest adventure with him was a trip to Colorado in the 1960s, also accompanied by my Aunt Lena and Uncle Lou. I vaguely remember playing piano, utterly terrified, at someone's beautiful home. The Colorado trip was a second foray beyond the "walls" of Illinois. The trip was mesmerizing because of the sheer, brilliant beauty of the state, the steep mountain roads I never had experienced before that initially terrified me because of Pete's Le Mans style of driving on the many switchbacks, and fishing on the South fork of the Platte River. Pete, like most of the Marino men, wanted always to get a "jump on the day," and that began at 4:00 a.m. each morning on this trip. What I remember was a freezing, dark day beginning that broke into sunshine over the mountains; we had been fishing already for several hours when breakfast (the trout we caught) was frying in a cast-iron pan over open flames, with coffee brewing and that river flowing through gifted scenery. Horses grazed nearby. All of this whetted my appetite to see more of this world.

Pete was charismatic, enjoyed his poker games, and loved a party. Uncle Nick, on the other hand, was quieter (if that was at all possible in this big, gregarious family); he was very tall and lanky, passing that on to one of my cousins who went on to play college ball. He, along with my Dad, became an electrician, and he had a successful career. Aunt Mary, one of the four Marino sisters, was a big woman—we would have called her "very peasant"; my memory may be faulty but I believe she was much bulkier and taller than Grace. She and Grace were the "sweatshop sisters," working in the garment industry for a good part of their lives. Mary could make symphonies out of flower sacks with her sewing. Like Grace, she spoke more broken than standard English, and their lives centered around home and hearth.

Mary was married to a dolt, someone never kind to her and not worthy of space here. (See, we weren't all one big happy family; we had our moments; we weren't naïve to the foibles and failures of us all as humans.) I remember there wasn't much of a conversation between Mary and her husband; it almost seemed like an arranged marriage. I often saw the divergence between the sisters Frances and Lena who went out into the world, and Mary and Grace who worked but mostly looked inward.

I haven't said much about the other side of my family, the Lithuanians who invaded Italy, when my Mom came to marry my Dad. Annie (Ann Helen) was beautiful, and in her youth was compared to Clara Bow, a 1920s actress known as the "It Girl." Annie learned cooking at the early age of 16, when she was absorbed into this big Italian family in the early 1920s, marrying my Dad at, I believe, 24. She had dark hair and dark eyes, although fair-to-medium skin, while her sister, Rose, one of my favorite aunts, had alabaster skin,

My mother in 1938

light blue eyes, and light brown hair that turned to silver gray when I was in my teens. We always joked that maybe the Mongol hordes had actually invaded their family and they'd had two different fathers.

Ann was the diplomat and Rose the "*sturm und drang*"—direct, opinionated, and like "Sherman's march to the sea" in arguments. She and my Dad locked horns every Thanksgiving and Christmas over politics, religion (she tagging my Dad a "Papist"), and food. Rose, a Lutheran, vehemently disliked Catholics because the nuns took away the *Lithuanian Daily Draugus* newspaper that my ailing Grandfather, Ignatz (better known as Harry), liked to read. Raised a Catholic, she never looked back on what she viewed as a tyrannical chokehold on reason. I remember her sending me a gift when I graduated from the University of Illinois, stating, "Finally, no more Catholic education!" A lighter subject at Thanksgiving was about the food. "Rose, you didn't cook the damn bird again and I don't like the green beans—they're

Aunt Rose

almost raw!" Dad would squawk. "Well, what would you know about cuisine and the best way to get vitamins from your veggies! Just eat the food; you're lucky you have food on the table!" Rose declared, giving it back to Alex, both barrels fully loaded.

Both women were intelligent and well read, Rose maybe more than my mother, who had to work in her later life while raising four children. Besides being a reader, Rose was self-taught and devoured everything from history to how to hook up a stove. She oversaw the expansion of her home, adding what we know today as a family room, getting in there and doing some of the work herself.

For her part, Annie taught herself how to run a school cafeteria, managing the menus, books, and Federal government supplies with her trusted sidekick, Agnes the cook. I remember how both Agnes and Ann balked at bringing in prepared frozen meals. They both cooked every day, five days weekly, to give their young charges a hot meal, sometimes giving them seconds if they had enough. I remember my mother telling me that federal regulations required dumping the supplies if they were not all used by the end of the week. My mother would regularly give food out the back door of the cafeteria to people who needed it. This Depression-era survivor said she would never just dump food, that the Feds could *put* her in jail. Annie was a woman who lifted heavy pots all day in that small kitchen, and also read Herman Hesse!

Both sisters stood their ground in the male-dominated world they encountered—Annie with the five very stubborn and often traditional first-generation Italian-American brothers-in-law she inherited, and

Rose in the world of sports that she inherited through being married to my Uncle Eddie, a sports columnist for the *Chicago Sun Times* and the old *Chicago Herald-Examiner* for 44 years before retiring in 1973. Uncle Eddie was the epitome of kindness, soft-spoken, a gentle, bright man, the son of a minister from Indiana—an interesting contrast to the often-explosive personalities of the Marino men. Both my mother and Aunt Rose were independent and incredibly strong—a strength forged, I believe, from their young lives having seen family alcoholism, illness, and tragedy, with two brothers dying at a young age.

They were all my family, my community; and how I still love each and every one of them to this day, with all their faults and fissures, but all their gifts and hearts. These were the first-generation sons and daughters of immigrants—people plopped into "middle earth," the Midwest, into the long road forged so long ago, in the 17th and 18th centuries, of "all men are created equal" with the right to pursue life, liberty, and happiness. I doubt very much that they were at all aware of their role in the great and necessary work of carrying on this Sacred Trust. Their contributions were the unmarked and unsung efforts of their daily lives: the homes they created; the education they gave to their children, in sending the next generation on to a better life in some respects; in the community of love and decency they built with each of their life's bricks, one by one.

These were the first "builders" of my character, of the person whom I have become. Each had their unique character, their own way of approaching life. I always carry with me the lessons I learned from them. But most especially, I carry the life lessons from my Dad, even though in my teenage and college years I wasn't as close to him as to my Mom. But looking back, it was my Dad's lessons that I have taken with me on my own journey.

CHAPTER 2

The Reckoning

Without one moment's questioning—no sizing me up—without missing a beat the two women listened to their hearts, and humanity spread around me like a warm coat on a cold day. There wasn't a moment of hesitancy in their outstretched arms. And for my part, I didn't dissect whether they were Muslim, Arab, Persian, or anything else. That hug and the warmth I received from those young women was so exquisitely human, the best of what we are as a species.

To understand more of the reckoning, I wanted to understand the roots of my own family's point in the history of America: the life my Dad, Alex, faced in his experience as a first-generation American in the face of prejudice against immigrants, both subtle and direct. I wanted to understand what my father had passed on to me, consciously or unconsciously, in the larger context of American history, and how these details ultimately influenced my concept of how we function in the world we live in today.

March was a blustery month that year of 2016, but with some beautiful sunny days. An old friend had suggested that we plant a tree in my late husband Al's memory. And so, on a Thursday morning, I decided to get in a short hike in the park near my home, which holds the memory of my late best friend and our walks in the redwoods, their giant canopies touching the sky above. It was, and continues to be, my place for solace and peace; a place where I can reclaim calm and quiet, and be disturbed only by the occasional hawk circling high above, or by rabbits with white cotton tails carefully climbing out of their bushy hiding places to get food. Al is always there for me, and I stop by one particular tree to place my hand on its welcoming wide bark, to pray and talk to my gone-away friend.

As I was hiking and getting deeper into those woods, I suddenly bent over with a gut-wrenching, deep, deafening sorrow that came over me, crying from my depths, losing my breath and howling from the hole left in my heart, a void beyond any abyss. It had been only nine months since my husband had passed away. When this finally ceased, I realized that I was bent over on my knees. I dusted myself off, wiped my face of tears, took a deep breath, and thrust myself forward on the path. I checked my watch and realized I would have to get back. The "tree planting" memorial ceremony was only two hours away, and I still needed to change out of my trail clothes.

I pressed forward along the bridal trail, a narrow sliver, parts of which were supposed to accommodate horses, hikers, bikers, and joggers—no mean trick on a busy weekend filled with families and friends getting together. But today, this early morning, the trail was almost empty, a reflection of my heart's void. Sadness followed me like a shadow down the trail, and the tears I tried holding back did not want to be left unreleased. My body was hiking, an almost out-of-body experience as I placed one foot after the other. But my *heart* and *soul* were in some other space, stopped in time by grief.

I really tried to keep my sorrow in its own subconscious room so I wouldn't feel the pain. But as the trail wound through trees, ivy, rocks, and brush down towards the Stream Trail, the tears began again. They were not having this "being under wraps" treatment. They needed to show themselves in that morning's mourning.

I was wiping away the tears as I entered the main trail heading back home, when two young women, probably in their late 20s, stopped me to ask where this particular trail led. Both, I could tell, were of Middle Eastern descent—Persian, Arab, I don't know. One wore a Hijab, one did not. Both had big dark eyes, dark hair.

I explained where the trails led. Stream lead straight into Mill, then took a sharp left and up to French Trail; the other led back into multiple trails, mostly uphill. As I was standing there explaining all my worldly knowledge of trails, one of the women, the one with the

Hijab, surprised me by asking, "Are you all right?" The other offered, "You look sad." To which the woman with the Hijab said, "You look like you could use a hug." And just like that, the two of them put their arms around me and gave me a good, strong, welcoming hug. It was just what I needed; I was, and still am, very lonely for my Al.

I wished them a good hike and sent them off with a hug in return. As they walked up the dirt trail, chattering happily, I was suddenly struck by the sheer humanity of that moment. Here were two perfect strangers, clearly Middle Eastern (maybe one more secular than the other who wore the Hijab), out enjoying an early morning hike. But what came out of them were two women seeing another woman, sad and lately of tears, who literally needed a hug. Without one moment's questioning—no sizing me up—without missing a beat they listened to their hearts, and humanity spread around me like a warm coat on a cold day. There wasn't a moment of hesitancy in their outstretched arms. And for my part, I didn't dissect whether they were Muslim, Arab, Persian, or anything else. That hug and the warmth I received from those young women was so exquisitely human, the best of what we are as a species, that I went home that morning knowing I could handle the tree-planting memorial service, with all its embedded emotional tug-of-war.

As I walked back to my car, I reflected on these two young women, and on how Muslims had become the new bogeyman under the Trump administration. Hispanics as a group had also been labeled, in that administration, as rapists, bringing drugs and crime. At various times throughout our history, different groups have been "tagged" as undesirable for political expediency, always using fear and chaos as the stick that stirs the pot. Sadly, the labeling isn't limited to this country or to this particular moment in time.

When I look back over history—not just Western Civilization, but also Asian, African, Latin American, you name it—I think of the colossal waste of time spent on wars, on the colonial passion for expansion driven by the need for power and economic aggrandizement. We as humans have probably wasted the talent, energy, and creativity of so many who have gone before. We spend an inordinate amount of time focused on division, whether by race, wealth, class, armies, land, religion, or other ways, that we are inclined to categorize and box us all in.

I know my Mother's Lithuanian family was not too happy about her marriage to an Italian, let alone a Sicilian. Definitely a step down for them; after all, the Lithuanians were Northern European, a cut above "those Mediterraneans." My father, however, only saw her beauty, her vivaciousness; he wasn't about to let that opportunity disappear. He looked beyond her label and saw Ann, the woman. This seems so inconsequential today, but in the late 19th and very early 20th century, those labels—"Bohunks," "Lugans," "Dagos," "Micks," "half-breeds," and some, like the "N" word, that have been carried forward into this century—were the tools of those who wanted to remain in power. Not having "Dagos" on the Chicago Police Force in the early days of the 20th century was a known fact. Probably because they were "different."

Labels, categories, boxes to contain and disempower groups of people have been used to sow fear and hatred for centuries, in the struggles for more wealth and power. That holds true for the dynasties of China's empires; the Pharaohs' Egypt; Rome's aggressive reach into the Eastern Mediterranean or the shores of Britain; the Spanish conquest of the Caribbean, of Central and Latin America; the Portuguese in Brazil; the tribal conflicts within Africa; and Native America long ago. Yet within those struggles for wealth and power, there has been a march towards individual rights, religious freedom, freedom from oppression—a need for humans to be judged not by their history or genealogy but by their talents. If someone wanted to be a writer and not the butcher's son, there might be a time and place where that could happen.

There were foundational steps, expanding (albeit slowly) to a larger portion of the population. The Magna Carta, issued in June 1215, is revered as a step towards individual rights, because it stated that the king and government are not above the law (even though, when originally drafted, its codification was mainly for the English aristocracy). But within that document were seeds that led to the growth of something we call *individual rights*. "By declaring the sovereign to be subject to the rule of law and documenting the liberties held by 'free men,' the Magna Carta provided the foundation for individual rights in Anglo-American jurisprudence."[3] And those who fled religious persecution from Europe in the 17th century and landed on

America's shores wanted a place in time to worship in peace without being persecuted.

The ideals embodied in the Constitution and the Declaration of Independence, as I see it, spring from diverse historical struggles. Religious freedom and separation of church and state, for example, resulted in part because of the political, financial, and religious hammer that the Catholic Church wielded for centuries in Europe, setting policies and fomenting wars, as well as because of the rise of Protestantism, which took its turn in hanging heretics and quelling rebellions of less reputable branches of the big P. The right of free speech is another concept emerging from absolute power crushing so many voices by brute force over the centuries in so many parts of the world, and to this day in places like North Korea. The freedom from arbitrary arrests codified in the Fourth Amendment sprang from the history of the search-and-seizure that was so common a practice in the ancient world going forward.

The Founding Fathers looked back at the human struggle over centuries to be free to choose one's destiny and not have it be proscribed by a certain group holding power within society. They reached into moments in history, such as the signing of the Magna Carta, which set forth the idea that nobles had certain liberties—free church, reforms of justice—and that the *king* was subject to a "rule of law," unheard of during the time of the "divine right of kings." The genius of these Founders' thinking is that they took the ideals of the Magna Carta and other concepts of liberty and expanded them to include "all men"—the butcher as well as the baron. They chose their words carefully to allow for a living language that not only described the need for this in the late 18th century, but also would provide flexibility for an ever-evolving nation. The language was both constant in its ideals and expansive to embrace the future.

While the architects of America's governing policies and philosophical stance set into motion a movement towards greater humanity, equity and access—"...all men are created equal, that they are endowed by their Creator with certain unalienable Rights, that among these are Life, Liberty and the pursuit of Happiness"—the reality of what was happening on the ground was in stark contrast to the ideal. The Puritans fled religious persecution in their own country to be able to pursue their faith as they saw it in this new land. There were those who escaped debtors' prison to start a new life, to build their future unfettered by old European concepts of debt. Others were fleeing political persecution. Yet at the same time that some Founders were extolling the virtues of individual freedom, they were also simultaneously importing slaves (primarily from Africa) to work their cotton plantations—presumably so they wouldn't have to pay for workers and could maximize their profits. While in the 17th and 18th centuries there was some attempt to live peacefully with Native Americans, those who had fled persecution in favor of the wilderness of America to build a better life created their own acts of injustice against Native Americans, robbing them of their lands and pushing them ever further westward. A further injustice was the overlay of European culture and identity on both the enslaved Africans and the Native Americans. This was a strategy to make them appear closer to white people by

Black Codes

24

having them adopt the clothing, food, and language of the Europeans in power, a game plan embraced even by George Washington. That strategy has left a stain on the country's ideals for over 300 years.

For Native Americans, broken treaties and promises were the hallmarks of the 17th through the early 20th centuries, and are still extant in the recent attempt to put a tar sands pipeline through sacred tribal lands in the Midwest. For African Americans, Reconstruction (that era from 1865-1877) or what it was meant to accomplish went terribly wrong. Although in the end, President Lincoln felt that enslaved peoples and those who had fought for the union should have the right to vote, he was assassinated before he could translate that into law. What followed were known as the "black codes," which criminalized behavior and restricted Blacks' labor in numerous ways—from forcing employers to pay low wages, to jailing Blacks who were jobless. Black people, for example, were required to sign annual labor contracts; and if they refused, they could be arrested, fined, or forced into unpaid labor.[4]

In 1867, there was a brief shining moment with the passage of the Radical Reconstruction Act, a response of the electorate to the egregiousness of the "black codes." There was a short interval after the black-code era where a modicum of social and political progress took place. African Americans were elected to Southern state legislatures and the U.S. Congress. Southern states had to ratify the 14th and 15th amendments (equal protection of citizenship and the right to vote for former enslaved people, respectively) as a requirement for acceptance back into the Union. Congress passed the first Civil Rights Act in 1866, and land seized by the Union army was to be redistributed to former enslaved people.

All of this was dismantled, except for the amendments under President Andrew Johnson, when conservative right-wing agents such as the Ku Klux Klan emerged and Johnson allowed the Southern states to reinvent themselves the way they wanted. White supremacy had emerged the victor by the 1870s. The elements of these "black codes were transformed into Jim Crow Laws."[5]

"Jim Crow laws were a collection of state and local statutes that legalized racial segregation. Named after a Black minstrel show character, the laws—which existed for about 100 years, from the post-Civil

First United States Black Senator and US Representatives, 1872. "First Colored Senator and Representatives," Smithsonian National Portrait Gallery. (Hiram Rhoades Revels, 27 Sep 1827–16 Jan 1901; Benjamin Sterling Turner, 1825–1894; Josiah T. Walls, 1842–1905; Joseph Harvey Rainy, 1832–1887; R. Brown Elliot, 1842–1884; Robert Carlos De Large, 1842–14 Feb 1874; Jefferson Franklin Long, 3 Mar 1836–5 Feb 1900)

War era until 1968—were meant to marginalize African Americans by denying them the right to vote, hold jobs, get an education, or other opportunities. Those who attempted to defy Jim Crow laws often faced arrest, fines, jail sentences, violence and death."[6] Jim Crow laws effectively kept African Americans in another form of slavery—poverty—until the Civil Rights Act of 1968.

Think about that—it is only in my lifetime that the dream of freedom has begun to emerge for this particular group of citizens. I relate that to how—after the Italian unification in the 1860s—the power, money, and legislative ability were concentrated in Northern Italy, which set the rules and funneled monetary and other support to the North, leaving much of Southern Italy in poverty. Sicily and Southern Italy only began to come into their own in the last decades of the 20th century. This striving for power and control over others seems to be the bane of human existence, stretching across time and continents.

Because the plight of both Native Americans and African Americans was never really addressed by the Founding Fathers and was derailed in the post-Civil War era, there is now a reconstruction reckoning occurring, one that spurs us to re-examine the American Dream. The only time that enslaved people "counted" was in the 3/5 compromise, when Southern states wanted them counted as 3/5ths of a person for representation and taxation purposes; but they weren't counted at all as human beings in any other situation in American history. How convenient and transactional for the Southern States! And Native Americans were, for all practical purposes, mostly non-existent.

To understand more of the reckoning, I wanted to understand the roots of my own family's point in the history of America: the life my Dad, Alex, faced in his experience as a first-generation American in the face of prejudice against immigrants, both subtle and direct. I wanted to understand what my father had passed on to me, consciously or unconsciously, in the larger context of American history, and how these details ultimately influenced my concept of how we function in the world we live in today.

Examining Alex's role as a first-generation Italian-American in Chicago has helped me to see more clearly how the American experiment has worked for some but not for everyone. We are on a long-delayed march towards this "… more perfect union" in the 21st century and what that means for all of us.

We have choices to make.

CHAPTER 3

The Setting of the Joy

Lessons from the
Alexander Francis School of Life

What I didn't understand as a 14-year-old was that I was, and already had been, in "Alex's school of life"—one of street smarts, absorbing his views and ways through the epidermis, to the ears, to the frontal cortex, to the heart, through hundreds of dinner-table conversations, eaves-dropping on adults when my parents had parties, or listening to pronouncements made to his wife.

Alex's journey gave me great gifts, and they were many: toughness; street smarts; a very attuned "bullshitometer"; understanding that life isn't always easy or fair, that sometimes things just don't work out; finding grit to pull yourself up when you've been knocked down, and to keep going; not complaining, because someone else will always have it worse than you; that imperfect, flawed people can often be instruments of good in spite of themselves; pragmatism as a necessary tool for problem solving; not being intimidated by power structures; understanding that just because something has lasted a long time doesn't necessarily mean it's right or infallible; and, perhaps, most importantly, the power of love.

The last of these, I learned not from his words—Alex wouldn't have expressed love or spent much time describing emotions or talking about feelings. No, it was in the hundreds of things over the years that he did....

It was June 1975, and I was finishing up a project in Sacramento for my new job when I got a phone call from my husband, Al. He had just gotten off the phone with my sister, and now was calling to tell me in a halting voice that foreshadowed those awful words, "PJ, your Dad had another heart attack. He's gone."

The drive home was a blur, the windshield made misty through the tears streaming down my face. My sobbing was interrupted by gulps of disbelief. I had just called my parents for their anniversary the week before and had missed my Dad by minutes. "That's all right," I had said to my Mom, "I'll see Dad next week." But next week never came. Now, the word "gone" had exclamation points surrounding it. In the years that followed, many of those who constituted my big family—all the aunts and uncles who'd had a hand in my formation—were also "gone," and most I could not personally say good-bye to because I now lived 2,000 miles away.

So, here I am 47 years later at the age of 75, taking into account how this man I called Dad formed me in no small way into who I am today, both directly and indirectly—what I have learned from him to exist in this world, which is so different in many ways from the world he grew up in, but in some ways the same. This is not to say that my Mom wasn't a huge influence, she was—but my Dad was unmistakably Alex! Whenever Mom and Dad were going out, Dad always had on his hat and, in winter, his camel overcoat. He always believed in looking smart; the hat made him look like writer Dashiell Hammett's 1930s-character, Sam Spade. On the other hand, he didn't look so smart come summer, when his Bermuda shorts came out and he would wear socks (on his long, skinny legs) that went almost to his knees—with tennis shoes!

Saying that Alex was gregarious was an understatement. He always had a huge smile, enjoyed his friends and family, and if he thought you had your head on straight, you probably received the moniker, "Buttercup"—that was his tag line for those he thought had good sense. Dad loved to dance, and at the regular "Guild" parties (a fundraising group—the term *guild* comes from medieval trade associations—for our church: Our Lady of the Heart Guild, I think it was), which rotated from house to house in the neighborhood, there was Dad behind the bar in our basement, music going, telling jokes and

Alex (far right) and friends

otherwise regaling folks with one of his Chicago Police detective stories or singing "Swanee" (yes, "Swanee")! I wanted to understand the gift of his essence, what he taught me both by his actions and his words—words from a man who didn't discuss emotions or deep feelings, a man of the early to mid-20th century. He was as far as you can get from being a *metro male*, that heterosexual, urban, capitalist male who spends time and money on his looks. But in the old days, they would have called him a "dandy," only this one had an urban vibe-edge to him.

We were like two warhorses in a constant battle of ideas and philosophy as I grew up, and this dynamic was exacerbated even more as I morphed into a teenager and young adult in the later 1960s. I loved Bob Dylan, the Beatles, and rock of any kind. One year, I took off for spring break to Ft. Lauderdale, which to Dad was like choosing to be a prostitute. We locked horns over a woman's place—him thinking that was in the kitchen, married, with kids; me wanting a career, and hating the restrictions placed on women, either culturally or legally. It really got to me that I couldn't keep my own name if I married, or that the only potential working roles for women were teacher, nurse, or secretary. All great careers, but I wasn't sure I fit any of those roles. Pretty confining. Alex didn't see it that way. To him, going to college for a woman had only one goal—to get your "MRS," find a rich guy, and marry him! His thoughts about "book learning" were a holdover from his often-contentious relationship with Uncle Larry, the "book-learner lawyer." Alex definitely was not the book type!

I was, to say the least, a considerable irritant to Dad, challenging the status quo. When I was newly graduated from college, I worked briefly in the early 1970s on the campaign for Dawn Clark Netsch, a Democrat for the state legislature. Alex thought that was a stupid waste of time, since it would not serve any real, "street" purpose to provide some support to the neighborhood; and besides, she was part of that independent, "clean" part of the Illinois Democrats that were at regular odds with the Democratic political machine. *What good would that do?* was Alex's thinking; the machine always dominated in elections.

My habit of asking questions also did not sit well with him. When the Monsignor of our local Catholic grammar school was teaching sex education (and already, I thought to myself as a cool 8th grader, older than God) and I asked him, "What could you possibly know about sex?"—to which he promptly hit me on the back with his shillelagh and sent me home—my Dad's response was: "Why can't you just keep your mouth shut and stop asking questions?"

What I didn't understand as a 14-year-old was that I was, and already had been, in "Alex's school of life"—one of street smarts, absorbing his views and ways through the epidermis, to the ears, to the frontal cortex, to the heart, through hundreds of dinner-table conversations, eaves-dropping on adults when my parents had parties, or listening to pronouncements made to his wife, Annie. Our parish clergy was often a topic of discussion in our household; and those discussions, as with many others, left an imprint on my young brain.

"Annie, I was talking to John today, the plumber at the parish. He was telling me that that young priest, you know the new one...."

"Oh, that really good-looking dark-haired one," piped up Ann.

"Yeah, I think so. Well, rumor has it that he is seeing some young woman. Can you believe that? I can only imagine what the Monsignor must think—right under his nose!"

"Well, I still think it's weird in some way that priests can't marry, just abnormal, I think!" Ann's voice rose in exclamation.

Because of this, my view of priests and nuns was never one of saints on pedestals, but that they all were just human beings, as flawed as the rest of us. I was to learn later that these frank discussions were not as common as I thought among other Catholic families, who perhaps chose to see the saint more than the sinner in the comings and goings of priests.

Alexander Francis, dubbed "Frosty" by my brother, already had silver-gray hair by the time I was beginning to awake to being *in* the world. The silver gray sat on a 6' 1" frame with hazel eyes. He had a great laugh and smile, matched by a volatile Sicilian temper that could erupt along a Richter scale from smoldering to a 9.6, depending on the occasion. In a photo of "The Guild Halloween" party on October 30, 1960, there is Dad holding his drink up high, grinning above the motley crew of costumed "vampires, Lincolns, JFKs, da Mayor" and more, holding court as though his "drink" arm were conducting a

The Guild Halloween Party—a fundraising group for our Parish (1960s)

symphony of friends in a great musical reverie. But the ease with which he "conducted" social gatherings belied his ability to get right to business, when needed—whether that was transforming the old coal bin in the basement into a storage cupboard using his construction skills, or managing a stakeout while on duty to catch a burglar. Alex was head, heart, and body. He was, as they say—formidable.

This is a reflection on the gifts of Alex's essence, how he equipped me to live in a world of turbulence and change. He was the son of immigrants. Their struggles may have been different from those of modern immigrants to a certain extent, happening at a time in the early 20th century, and with his ancestry being from a Southern European nation not high on any WASP American dream list of acceptable "citizens" who fit the myth of what it meant to be an American. In the 1940s, the homes in the Cambridge Avenue neighborhood of Chicago owned by Italians were demolished to make room for public housing. I wonder: perhaps if these homes had been in a more upper-middle-class neighborhood owned by Northern Europeans, it might have been a different story. Yet the story of Alex and his parents, my grandparents, is one of many in the long march towards a just world that, today, is seeing a reckoning for the first and the last of those immigrants—descendants of African enslaved people who, because of skin color and their past as "owned property," are still in the process of assimilation; and Native Americans, who became a vanishing peoples in a monumental land grab.

Alex's journey gave me great gifts, and they were many: toughness; street smarts; a very attuned "bullshitometer"; understanding that life isn't always easy or fair, that sometimes things just don't work out; finding grit to pull yourself up when you've been knocked down, and to keep going; not complaining, because someone else will always have it worse than you; that imperfect, flawed people can often be instruments of good in spite of themselves; pragmatism as a necessary tool for problem solving; not being intimidated by power structures; understanding that just because something has lasted a long time doesn't necessarily mean it's right or infallible; and, perhaps, most importantly, the power of love.

The last of these, I learned not from his words—Alex wouldn't have expressed love or spent much time describing emotions or talking about *feelings.* No, it was in the hundreds of things over the years that he did, like picking up my friends and me in one of Chicago's inevitable snowstorms one evening as we were waiting for the bus to go home. There was Dad, who, after working all day, had trekked out in a blizzard to pick us up. It was dark, we had stayed at high school late; but he had braved that arctic wind ("the hawk") and slippery streets, and come out to drive us home. And he was there for my piano recital at Greenbriar Park, a big deal for a young girl. His love was there in the sausages or pasta (he would have called it "spaghetti") that he stopped to fetch for us on his way home.

The love also was obvious one night, in a truly funny Keystone Cops type of incident (those lovable, incompetent policemen featured in slapstick silent comedies from 1912 to 1920). One night, the place was lit like a Wrigley Field opener, both upstairs and downstairs in our two-flat. I remember it was a gathering of the clan, the relatives and some friends, though I cannot remember for what occasion. But every light was on, and the house was busy with plates clattering as people were getting food, with music playing, with the adults enjoying Manhattans, scotch, Rob Roys, and with kids running up and down the staircase.

I believe it was my Aunt Mary who went into one of the bedrooms to get something, when she noticed two hands on the first-floor windowsill. Some of the windows were half open to let the summer night breeze in. The two hands were attached to a body trying to lift himself up into the room. My Aunt screamed and ran to get my Dad and brother, both of whom scrambled up the stairs to the second floor to get the two shotguns that hung on our small den wall that only came down when my brother went hunting. Dad raced to get the bullets into the guns (I recall they had a hard time finding the bullets); and by the time the two of them raced down the stairs to the bedroom on the first floor, Aunt Mary was standing by the window, which now had *bluish-red* hands sticking out from its base, where she had slammed the window down on the perp's hands. Alex, the seasoned cop, and my brother, the seasoned hunter and ex-Marine, arrived on the scene just in time to "help" Aunt Mary the seamstress with their strong arms! Not a shot was fired!

Everyone had a good laugh that evening about Mary turning the tables on my Dad and brother. While it was Aunt Mary who had saved the day, I saw the love and concern for the safety of all of us in that scramble to get the guns, in not thinking twice about protecting the family. Now, to be sure, Alex may not have recognized these traits or tools or been able to describe them; but with every fiber of his being he lived them, as well as a larger treasury of gifts (to be demonstrated much more dimensionally in later chapters).

LESSON #1: Laws Don't Always Equal Right

A Portrait of Dirty Harry

So who was this character, Alexander Francis? For a character he was. To me, he was a cross between Dirty Harry, Frank Sinatra, and LBJ—an amalgam of street sense, fairness, savvy, brashness, and self-awareness.

He was a first-generation Italian-American seeking the American dream, seeking assimilation—most of which he attained, but probably to a lesser degree than what he desired. My Dad's view of the American Dream was, of course, to have enough money to support his family—a nice house and car, and to not have a money "anvil" over his head all the time in terms of monthly bills—nothing out of the ordinary for most children of immigrants, or for any middle- or working-class Americans. More than that, though, he wanted a better, easier life for his children (which, in his mind, perhaps included my marrying someone with wealth). I have found—in the many paths I have taken in my life with a myriad of people from diverse ethnicities, religions, and backgrounds—that wanting a better life for one's children seems a universal thread. Alex would not have used the term "American Dream," but in his actions, he spoke it. His rise from beat cop to detective in a relatively short time period demonstrated his commitment to get ahead.

He was a bright man, exceptional with math, educated at one of Chicago's great vocational high schools (as they were then called), not the more common Workforce Readiness (as it's called today), Lane Tech High School. His language was often riddled with cuss words, which rolled off his tongue like a primary language. "Son of a bitch!" was a favorite, along with "goddamn" and "goddamn bastard." Although I never ever heard the F-bomb, which I am sure he probably used when on the Chicago Police Department or with his co-workers.

Alexander Francis was a man of the 1920s to late 1950s. His bouts with angina and his heart attacks prevented him from continuing to work with his brothers' electrical business and, never really recovering material success, he became "locked" in that 30-year era whose descriptors ranged from bootleg and organized crime, to ragtime and flappers, to the Great Depression and World War II. These were the years of Dad's youth and young adulthood through his early 40s. My sense is that in the 1960s, as the social upheaval in the country took hold with Vietnam protests and the civil rights movement (and this now is memory talking, which may be clouded), Alex looked back to that earlier era in which he came of age to find some sense of familiarity, some order in his mind: the way things used to be. "Patty Jo, turn off that damn music! It's garbage!" he would yell when my Motown or the Kingston Trio (hardly gritty lyrics) would really irritate him. His love was for the music of Glen Miller, Frank Sinatra ("It's a Quarter to Three"), Ragtime, Rosemary Clooney, Perry Como, Bing Crosby—*real* music, which he thought clashed with my "pretend music." Bob Dylan's music would send him straight into a vitriolic recitation about how the world was really disintegrating!

The Dirty Harry part of his nature, I am sure, came from his time on the Chicago Police Department working vice, prostitution, homicide, and more. It also perhaps came from growing up in a transplanted Italian, nee Sicilian, village on the Near North side of Chicago, steeped by his immigrant parents in Sicilian culture, food, language, and interactions with others just like him. Eastwood's portrayal of Dirty Harry, the police officer, was of someone irreverent who often skirts the rules to get the job done, who was not afraid of bullies, con men, or gangsters. Sicilians are, if anything, determined, persevering, quick to call out hypocrisy.

There is a family story that Uncle Larry—who was a young attorney in the City Corporation Council, aka, a City attorney—was picked up by Al Capone or his minions (late 1920s) in a black limousine and driven around for a good part of the day. They kept asking him to

work for Capone, to which Uncle Larry kept saying, "Don't you understand; I work for the City Attorney's office." To which the minions
supposedly replied, "Yes, that's why we want you." They let him go;
but I remember the old ladies in the family saying, years later, that he
still broke out in a sweat when a black limousine passed by. Another
such legend (which may, as my brother says, be the "old ladies telling
tales") is of Uncle Larry doing some work for a cheese company in
Wisconsin. I remember how, many times, he would bring back balls
of provolone cheese wrapped in traditional heavy string to hang in
our basement. Supposedly, he found out that this was a front for one
of the mafia families, and then went to tell them that he wasn't having
anything to do with representing them any longer, nor anything to do
with them, period. He told my father to call the FBI if he wasn't back
in four or so hours, because that would mean he was dead. Fiction
or fact, I don't know; but these "rumors" suggest that standing up to
thugs seems to run in the family.

Chicago is and has remained a series of interconnected neighborhoods, with their distinct markings—and in my father's day, definitely
divided and defined by ethnicity, from Germantown to Andersonville
to Bucktown to Greektown and more. The "others" also included kids
who would grow up into members of the Chicago mafia. There was
no avoiding them, but there was a choice of not participating. There is
family "lore" that my grandmother took a broom to a mob underling,
telling him where he could go when he was depositing a body in the
street near the family home. She made her choice known.

Jane Addams began Hull House, a settlement house in early
20th-century Chicago, to help those downtrodden folks who came to
America's shores seeking that glittering and often elusive American
Dream. This woman who developed the career of social work reached
out to Italian immigrants with both compassion and a respect for
others' culture; her research into injustices against immigrants broke
ground in helping to develop a more enlightened approach to helping immigrants transition to their new home. However, the first half
of the 20th century was a time with no affirmative action for college
entrance (even if one could go to college) or for jobs; no nonprofit
organizations helping you get training to find work, no legal aid to
right a wrong from perhaps someone who had screwed you out of an

honest day's labor. No, this was an era of "pulling yourself up by your bootstraps." It was a time when you relied heavily on family support, on your neighbors, on the community that often formed around your church, your school. And this immigrant approach to survival continues to be one repeated even today, where reliance is always first on whom you know and can trust and speaks your language.

Alex learned toughness at an early age, working alongside his brothers during the day and going to high school at night to put their eldest brother, Larry, through college and then, law school—unheard of in those days for a first-generation son of not-so-welcomed "darkie" (Sicilian) immigrants.

My Dad also learned that sometimes rules get bent and that there are gradations of bending, depending on the rule and who benefits from the bending. Born in 1908 and just 21 when the Great Depression hit, Alex worked many jobs during this time, anything to put food on the communal table. He worked construction and WPA projects (Works Progress Administration projects were established in 1935 by President Franklin Delano Roosevelt to address the Depression and lack of jobs), but he also ran errands and clerked for his older brother, Larry the Lawyer. Along with his younger brother, Pete, he ran booze during Prohibition to judges and other City officials—"packages," as they liked to call it. The brothers made decent money until Larry the Lawyer put an end to that gig. Larry was about the rule of law, upholding the letter of the law, a by-the-book straight arrow. He abhorred any bending. Alex, on the other hand, saw some bending of the rules with this job—after all, judges were supposed to be upholding the law! But he also saw the stupidity and almost irrationality of some laws, such as Prohibition and its unintended consequences, giving a lucrative lifeline to the already existing Chicago mob, making them even stronger and wealthier. Lesson #1—Some laws are good, some—not so much. Laws do not always mean right.

> Although the temperance movement, which was widely supported, had succeeded in bringing about this legislation [the 18th Amendment], millions of Americans were willing to drink liquor (distilled spirits) illegally, which gave rise to bootlegging (the illegal production and sale of liquor) and speakeasies (illegal,

secretive drinking establishments), both of which were capitalized upon by organized crime. As a result, the Prohibition era also is remembered as a period of gangsterism, characterized by competition and violent turf battles between criminal gangs.[7]

While my grandparents and their children—my Dad and his siblings—were not "dirt poor" and were surrounded by a big family of 10, growing up as an Italian-American in the 1910s and 1920s in Chicago was not easy. The toughness was formed not just by work but also by the perception that Southern European immigrants were basically one step above African Americans, who were viewed as not just second class but as no-class.

Rumor has it that Richard J. Daly, the last of the Irish-ward bosses in American politics, put the Italians just in front of the Blacks in the annual St. Patrick's Day parade because "da mayor" allegedly despised both equally. The Chief of Police purportedly wrote a letter to the Mayor in the late 1920s or early 1930s on official City of Chicago stationery, stating that no Dagos need apply for positions with Chicago PD because we have enough of the "good lads" to fill the jobs.

For any immigrant or first-generation child of immigrants, growing up in that era meant literally making your own way. This was true for those who came before them and for those who are yet to come in this era. One always looked for who could help you progress, whatever defined achieving that American Dream. For most, that dream was one of material wealth and creating a better life for one's children. I am sure it was Alex's dream and what drove him.

The prejudice he encountered and his ability to overcome that and create a life for himself and eventually his family made him tough, a problem-solver, and a non-whiner. The prejudice was not from his peers and certainly not in his neighborhood, as the family moved to the Northside of Chicago. It was more what he encountered as a young man in the neighborhood of Little Sicily, known as "Little Hell," where other European transplants viewed Sicilians as less than desirable. It was also from his time on the police force, which was controlled in large part by the Irish; but his abilities enabled him to move up the ranks despite their "not needing more Dagos." I suspect that what formed his worldview and subsequent prejudices was the

Laws don't always equal right

fact that he had to go out into the world and figure out how it worked and how to succeed in it without much support or direction other than from his own family. He was no different from those who, every day, still struggle to do just that—craft a life from whole cloth.

There is this cultural perspective of "no one helped me," "I did this by myself"; and there were few, if any, social services available to soften the blow. Thus, when people like Alex see others who have had much more provided to them to "get ahead," an unconscious resentment forms—"Why *them*??" "Why did *I* have to struggle?"—that rests somewhere in the underbelly of a lot of prejudice. As we as a country have matured in some ways to recognize that immigrants and others in society need help, and that we need to provide that help (whether translation services, legal aid, health care, counseling, or affirmative action), such resentment can turn to anger—"Why not *me?*"—become bitterness, and devolve into prejudice.

That resentment is stoked even more when the American Dream, as defined by material success, slips away through no fault of the holder of that Dream.

LESSON #2: Call Out Hypocrisy

Alex and Sinatra

While the Dirty Harry character was certainly an aspect of Alex's character, some of Frank Sinatra's persona was dancing and singing its way through part of Alex's personality. A documentary I watched on Frank Sinatra's life[8] made it evident that he was a complex person. His Italian background, his surroundings in Hoboken, New Jersey, how he spoke with expletives all reminded me of Alex—the hardscrabble veneer they both had that often belied a very good heart.

What surprised me about Sinatra, and what I never had known before watching the documentary, was the fight for civil rights that he took on personally, early in his career. Sinatra remarked how, when he was growing up, everyone in his neighborhood went to public school—except the Blacks, who were relegated to the poorest area of Hoboken. He said he saw a few Blacks at school, but hardly any. Sinatra also said he didn't know much about racism until he went on the road for his musical career. He saw first-hand how Black entertainers were treated—prevented from coming through the front entrance to theatres by signs that read, "No Coloreds Allowed." This prejudice existed not only in some small Southern towns but also in New York City. It confounded him that Blacks could play in the orchestra or go on stage, but not be allowed to stay in the same hotels, eat at the same restaurants, or use the front doors. He wisely noted that most of a Black person's life was "from the backdoor entrance." Interestingly, Sinatra made a short film in 1945 called "The House I Live In" about racism, which was unusual at that time for a white person, let alone a white entertainer.

Frank Sinatra spent his lifetime fighting racism, but according to the documentary he did succumb to Joe Kennedy's request to *not* invite Sammy Davis, Jr., Sinatra's entertainer-friend, to the newly elected President Kennedy's inaugural ball. Davis had worked to get out the

Laws don't always equal right

Call out hypocrisy

vote in Black communities for Jack Kennedy. The crime he had committed? Davis had recently married Mai Britt, a tall, blond Swedish woman. Sinatra acquiesced to the senior Kennedy's request and told Davis he was not invited. Interesting that it appears the senior Catholic Kennedy, who went to Mass daily, was OK with Blacks voting for his son, but not with interracial marriage.

Alex had a great disregard for wealthy people who were cheap. But the greater sin, to him, was hypocrisy, whether political, personal, or religious. He despised Joseph P. Kennedy, and always said that he allegedly made his money in bootlegging using his money and power to invariably bend the rules to fit the Kennedy "plan." The bootlegging subsequently has been debunked in David Roos' October 28, 2019 article, "How Joe Kennedy Made His Fortune (Hint: It Wasn't Bootlegging)."[9] While Alex was wrong about Joe Kennedy, his take on hypocrisy is still a useful benchmark. "Patty," he would growl, "you don't have to worry about the guys who look weird or strange; they're telling you what they are about. Watch out for the ones in black tie, polished shoes, and who are educated. They'll smile at you while they are sticking a knife in your back"—Lesson #2 in Alex's school of hard knocks. While my Dad wanted all the trappings of the American Dream, I am sure—nice car, big house, a good business that says you've made it—he did not brook hypocrisy or people trying to "lord" it over others just because they had money.

Lesson #2—Call out hypocrisy even when it is difficult or may cost you something of value, whether tangible or intangible. The price for not addressing hypocrisy can be a heavier one than losing the valued thing.

LESSON #3: Mixing With the Mob Is a Death Knell

Alex and Sinatra

Sinatra's connection to the mob was never proven, but it was suspected. There is some research to indicate that Joe Kennedy contacted Sinatra to have him use his connections to the mob to deliver the Chicago and West Virginia votes.

It's interesting that Alex had similar characteristics to Sinatra—from his brashness to his sense of fairness—but the similarities end with mob connections. While he certainly knew some people in the mob, growing up, he was well aware of the grotesque nature of their work and the finality of their required commitment.

A case in point. One summer day when I was about eleven, Alex had to deliver something to a posh suburb of Chicago—River Forest, as I recall, but it might have been elsewhere. As we were driving past some of the mini-mansions with their pristine landscapes, he pointed to one mansion on steroids and said, "See that house, Pattie? That's Sam Giancana's home. Now, remember, you never want to get mixed up with these guys. The only way out is in cement shoes in the Chicago river." Duly noted, Dad.

Lesson #3—a good equation to learn: mob = life sentence divided by death! Another lesson in street smarts: avoid the mob at all costs, otherwise, you are not long for this world. Clear, direct, and surgically precise, as only Alex could be.

He and Sinatra would have recognized each other, for some of their characteristics certainly overlapped—the cursing and toughness, the intransigence about the way to do things, the "ready-to-do-battle" mentality. But also, the heart and the caring. Alex was a fan of Sinatra's music, from the late 1930s through the early 1960s.

Alex's love of music also showed up in his paying for my piano lessons, probably when I was 8 or 9—primarily so I could play for his poker parties. And I did play for many of them. He was always perplexed that my piano teacher gave me classical lessons, since Debussy was as foreign to him as Glenn Miller was a welcome friend. Alex not only loved music but was also a great dancer—that's how he met my mother—at a dance in downtown Chicago. His love of music brought him together with Blacks on somewhat more of a social level. When he was on the Chicago Police Department, he and his partner, a fellow detective, would sometimes go to what was called the "Black and Tan" clubs on Chicago's Southside—a place in that very segregated city where whites and Blacks mixed through the vehicle of entertainment.

Between 1923 and World War II, Chicago was the jazz capital of the world thanks to the Great Migration, which brought thousands of African Americans from the Deep South to the South Side. More than 70 nightclubs, ballrooms, and theatre halls lined the streets of Bronzeville—particularly along a stretch of State Street known as "the Stroll" from 31st to 39th Streets—where Nat King Cole, Louis Armstrong, Cab Calloway, Earl Hines, Jelly Roll Morton, and King Oliver all came of age, often in clubs owned and controlled by Al Capone.

Sadly, "the Stroll" was demolished after World War II to make way for Mies van der Rohe's Illinois Institute of Technology campus, and the grand venues on King Drive—the Regal Theatre and the Savoy Ballroom—were replaced by the Harold Washington Cultural Center.... Later renamed the Grand Terrace Cafe when Al Capone bought a 25 percent stake, this [The Sunset Café] "black-and-tan" (integrated) jazz club was one of the most important venues in the history of music. It's where Earl "Fatha"

Hines and Louis Armstrong made a name for themselves playing duets in the mid-'20s. A few years later, it's where Cab Calloway and Nat King Cole landed some of their first professional gigs alongside legends like Count Basie, Dizzy Gillespie, Charlie Parker, Sarah Vaughan, and even Benny Goodman.[10]

At a time of Jim Crow and overt and covert racism, here were places of respite from segregation where folks of all "stripes" could just enjoy the music. I am interpreting here, but I can see my Dad looking beyond the color barrier and "seeing" the music, the talent. At those perennial poker parties where my piano playing was put to use, Alex would make me "grasshoppers," a popular trendy cocktail in those days, but mine were filled with ice cream and milk and a tinge of crème de menthe for color. As I grew older, the ice cream dissolved into something more adult. The piano playing gave me an appreciation for the music of the early 1900s through the 1950s—Cole Porter, Satchmo Armstrong, Glen Miller, Sinatra, and so many others. The jazz, ragtime, and blues of that timeframe still live in my brain, along with Chopin and Tchaikovsky. These poker parties were a window into the world of adults, the issues in our parish, the comings and goings of political wannabees, gadflies, and ward bosses.

"Charlie, did you hear that story about Hanrahan [the Monsignor] today?" Alex asked as he perused his poker hand in a 5-card stud game.

"What are you talking about?" chirped the Judge, Bob O'Connor, another inveterate player in this monthly neighborhood game.

"Well, the City wanted to make that corner of Fairfield and Bryn Mawr a right-angle curve. So do you know what the son-of-a-bitch Hanrahan wanted? A curved corner, no right angles for him!" laughed Alex. "But what was even better was that they had to check where utilities were running. And when the line guys were checking the meters, they found out that the parish has been on the City's line for years!! So the Church has been getting off without paying a dime!" Alex's voice rose with the exclamation.

"Yeah, so what's new in Chicago?" O'Connor declared, shuffling the deck for another hand.

Laws don't always equal right

Call out hypocrisy

Beware of the mob mentality of fascism

"Nothing new," Alex said, "but true to form, the damn utilities guys said they weren't going to change anything. If the City wasn't raising a stink, then they wouldn't either!"

Interesting discussions like this floated around the cards and into this "little human" piano-player's ears, who somehow had disappeared into the wall and wasn't noticed much by the band of brothers around the poker table in our dining room. And so I had an early education into how things worked in Chicago.

But Sinatra and my Dad probably parted ways over racism. Sinatra came out early in the 1940s or early 50s with a commercial he made for youth and teens about bullying and racism, talking about being different and respecting each other—highly unusual for that time, especially coming from a white person. And for the rest of Sinatra's life, he saw racism as stupid and illogical. Alex, on the other hand, was definitely a man of his time. His view was the view of many whites at that time: struggling to keep Blacks at arms-length and, in the case of home ownership, a city-wide distance relegating African Americans to the South and Southwest sides of Chicago. As the 1960s came into view, I remember how seeing Blacks in downtown Chicago caused a shiver down some white folks' spines, that somehow this wasn't right, that State Street would soon be going downhill. My foggy memory includes a reminiscence (one my brother says he doesn't recall and maybe didn't happen) that good Catholics in our neighborhood (along with, I presume, good Protestants and who knows who else) prevented an African American judge from purchasing a home in our neighborhood. The irony of Jesus' words about loving our neighbors and enemies alike seemed not to cause anyone to think twice about their protests on African American ownership.

While Sinatra was on point with racism, his alleged association with some of the "outfit" clouded the other part of his legacy. Lesson #3—Mixing with the mob could mean you might wear some rather heavy shoes in water—not a good combination. While this is a literal lesson that might not apply to all people and circumstances, an extension of this concept is learning to make good choices, including choosing the company you keep. My Dad was protective, having seen the darker side of human beings from his days as a detective. He knew that wrong associations could lead to that darker side of the street that no one should walk.

LESSON #4: Strive to Learn Toughness through Adversity

Alex and Working the System

So, yes, Alex was a man of his time—which is not to excuse him but to understand him. He was prejudiced in the macro. Yet when I would mention Lou at Losby's Drugstore, a fixture in our neighborhood for many years—a quiet, soft-spoken African American man who would work for Harold Losby for many years—my Dad said he was "different." Interpretation—he was acceptable. Alex at least saw the man's humanity. And, at the end of his life, when the American Dream had slipped away for my Dad and his final job before retiring was working for AFDC (Aid to Families with Dependent Children), he saw the injustices of a system that sometimes was not very fair to those it was purporting to help. He would talk about the families he helped "work the system" so that they had a better chance of surviving. Again, the bending of the rules—but I think my father saw how the rich and powerful bent those rules all the time, and he wondered why it was "inappropriate" for those lower down on society's ladder to do the same; why they alone were held to the letter of the law.

Alex's prejudices were not limited to Blacks. His views of women were easily out of the 19th century when he told me that women, biologically, could only go so far. I know he loved my mother, but his view of women was as the helper, sidekick, and all things related to the home.

Thankfully, my mom was not one to be bullied or put in her place. My sister had trouble with reading and academics; today we would call it learning disabilities. I remember my mother getting on a bus with my sister, and going on that 45-minute ride to downtown Chicago to get the help my sister needed with her disability. My father would always wonder why she was spending this money and taking all that time. Wouldn't it be better to just stay in the neighborhood, and find a good "Italian" tutor or doctor to help? (Dad being the first-generation son of an Italian immigrant, naturally he thought of an Italian for help.) My mother would have none of that, and my sister is the better for it. Mom worked hard all her life, not only raising four children but also adapting to life in a huge Italian-American family (after all, she was Lithuanian and not from nearly the same background as my father's family), learning Italian for the sake of survival, and learning to cook like an Italian (and she did it well). She also faced having to go to work at the local school cafeteria to make ends meet when my father had a series of heart attacks and was unable to help with his brothers' electrical contractor's business. Even then, she was still expected not only to cook but also to entertain and clean, as well as work. Luckily, childcare wasn't an issue, because my aunts and uncles and cousin in the flat right below were always there to help.

I remember quite vividly the time in 1972 when Alex was talking to my new husband of two years about law school; Dad thought he had caught the brass ring, with a future lawyer in the family. At the time, I was in a Master's program while working. During this discussion, he turned to me and said, "Why the hell do you need to have a

PhD? That's just stupid!" I could not believe what he had said about my mother, about women in general, and about me, specifically—what he thought a woman's place should be. This led to an explosion of expletives from me against my Dad. When my father—shocked that words like "MF" and "shit" came out of my mouth—asked, "Where did you learn such language?" I replied, "From you, you goddam son of a bitch, for the last 27 years listening to it!"

I knew that my Dad loved me; but he was formed by the household he had grown up in, by living within the framework of his familial and city culture and the America of his time. His love showed in picking me up from school on really cold winter nights if I stayed late; in being overprotective of me in terms of who I was dating; and in making sure that we enjoyed good-quality food every day, not just for special occasions, because he thought that even if you don't have a grandiose budget there should be some quality in your life.

While I wasn't happy with him at all and didn't recognize his value in the moment, his toughness, strength, and life-lesson pedagogy gave me the toughness and grit to give it back to him in spades. He gave me the gift of not being intimidated by anything or anyone older, with more power or strength. And his intransigence about women and others not of the same ilk developed in me a greater sense of the need for people to be who they are meant to be, to view *humans as humans*—not based on their gender, race, or creed, but on who they are as people.

Of course, his views on women informed mine in those early '70s days that coincided with the women's movement—a movement I felt was long overdue, not just in this country or even for the past 200 years, but for the millennia of time in every corner of the earth where women were and continue to be marginalized. *What a waste of human talent, energy, and skill*, I always thought. *Why not use all that to bring to bear on the problems of the world, much of which are borne by women?*

Lesson #4—I gained toughness from watching my father get knocked down by life and get back up despite adversity, from his continuing to put food on the table through four and then five heart attacks, which really curtailed his ability to do heavy work. His health issues affected the family's financial health, but Alex just kept going. I also learned how *not* to be intimidated by direct, strident arguments anchored in cultural mores of another place and time (Cambridge Avenue). My Dad and I vehemently disagreed about women's roles and the places in which people of a different skin color or culture should remain. Years later, when I was working for a Fortune 500 corporation, when senior management would remark that I didn't seem to be intimidated by titles, seniority, or comments made, I would always chuckle and say, "They always use that 'corporate diplomatic language,' which is sometimes smooth and belying 'the punch.'" Little did they know that I had gone up against the best—aka Alex—who always "took off the gloves" in his arguments and gave it to you with both barrels loaded. Having grown tough from that family treatment, I found corporate-world toughness to be no match for what I had gained by sparring with my Dad.

Laws don't always equal right

Call out hypocrisy

Beware of the mob mentality of fascism

Strive to learn toughness through adversity

LESSON #5: Keep Your Commitments

Alex and LBJ

Despite these obvious flaws, there was also in Alex elements of the character of LBJ—Lyndon Baines Johnson, the 36th president of the United States. No, I am not conflating my Dad's achievements with any of LBJ's (and there were many), but rather with the force of Johnson's *presence*.

> [LBJ] became known for his domineering personality and the "Johnson treatment," his aggressive coercion of powerful politicians to advance legislation. Despite Johnson's escalation of the Vietnam War, as Vice President and President he had a long list of accomplishments [from]...not support[ing] the 1956 Southern Manifesto, written to oppose racial integration to...supporting the creation of NASA (National Aeronautics and Space Administration); [he] coalesced votes for the passage of both the Civil Rights Act of 1964 and the Voting Rights Act of 1965; crafted the "Great Society" legislations to pass Medicare... appointed the first African American, Thurgood Marshall, to the Supreme Court;...and more.[11]

Alex's similarities to LBJ were more about his dominant personality and his uncanny ability to co-opt and coalesce people around an issue that needed resolving. He had a political savviness—innate, pragmatic, and realistic. While he wasn't officially a democratic precinct captain, he might as well have been, since he had a broad knowledge of the neighborhood. I often wondered if he was really a closet Republican, since he would not have supported an array of social safety nets. But one could not really function effectively in Chicago politics or gain access to city jobs or contracts if one wasn't both a Democrat and part of that all-encompassing machine, with its minions of cogs getting out the vote.

Alex knew just about everyone in the neighborhood—what today is Ward 40 on the political map—not just his small circle of church or business associates or friends. That meant he also knew well the local Precinct Captain, part of whose role would have been to ensure that the garbage was collected on time, and that constituents received new trash cans conveniently timed right before an election. One thing that used to be the hallmark of the Chicago political machine was that things basically worked for the everyday Joe. There was an unwritten law that the basics had to be taken care of if one were to get re-elected. And while Chicago was and maybe still is notorious for voting early and often (which sounds like the Trump administration's alleged modus operandi of doing anything to win), there was the recognition that given the right circumstances, public opinion could actually coalesce against you and you could be thrown out of office. So garbage pickup, trash-can deliveries, street sweeping, good parks and recreation areas—things the common people needed to sustain the common good—were, for the most part, attended to.

I know my Dad was savvy enough to stay close to local politics and what was going on in the ward, and I suspect it was definitely to support his outreach for his brothers' electrical contracting business. He even took his turn managing the political campaign of Otto, our local butcher, for Alderman. Alex saw firsthand the highs and lows of Chicago politics and sometimes statewide politics. He had an uncanny ability to get out the vote, and he made sure that everyone voted who could.

This may be once again "the old ladies talking" (a family folktale), but my memory recalls a story relayed by my mother. (My brother says he doesn't recall this, but I will relay it anyway.) One time, Alex and an old friend were asked to help deliver the vote in Kane County (the next-door neighbor to Cook County, home to Chicago) for then-Governor Kerner's re-election. Knowing my Dad, I suspect that something had been promised to him. For Alex, a deal was a deal was a deal. He did not brook reneging on a deal. I laughed when he was furious that I hadn't kept an exact tally list of who had given what gifts for my wedding, since he wanted to know both how to repay the "giftor" when the time came and who had met his measure of having been repaid for the many gifts and help he had given to a wide swath of neighbors, friends, and relatives.

Alex had the ability to read people and politics, understanding what mattered on the very basic level—how many new trash cans would a resident get? would they see better, faster garbage pickup?—the everyday items that mattered to the average person. What form that took in Kane County, I have no idea. The turnout for Kerner was strong in Kane County, so Alex and his sidekick, Don, did a good job. As a result, they were invited to the Governor's ball in Southern Illinois. In this "folktale reminiscence" of mine, Alex found out that whatever had been promised to him by Kerner's minions (I am sure my Dad never dealt with Kerner directly) had gone by the wayside—a definite reneging on the deal. Much to my mother's chagrin, my Dad took Kerner to task, calling him out on not keeping up his side of the bargain, and publicly telling him that—despite his blueblood credentials and Northwestern law degree—his administration would probably go down hard, because his Secretary of State, Paul Powell, had been committing fraud. My Mom was mortified that Alex had confronted the Governor publicly, but it turned out he was right.

Powell's effrontery was known as "The Shoebox Scandal,"[12] because over $750,000 was discovered in a shoebox, attache´ case, and other places. While some of the funds may have been legitimate, a court case revealed that Powell had taken bribes and kickbacks around horse racing and the production of state license plates. He infamously said, "There's only one thing worse than a defeated politician and that's a broke one."[13] His estate, once settled, was estimated to be around $3.5 million. Interesting for a politician on an annual public salary of about $30,000. Powell served in office from 1965-1970.

Democratic Governor Otto Kerner, himself, was later convicted of taking racetrack stock under the table, while also setting key racing dates for the Arlington Park racetrack (the Governor could do this, since he appointed the racing board that set the race schedule). Kerner went on to be convicted in 1973 of conspiracy, tax evasion, and perjury, although some charges were overturned on appeal. He spent three years in federal prison. A sad end to someone with a great career in the law, in politics, and in service to his country in World War II.

Alex saw up close and personally the hypocrisy of public officials who had sworn to uphold their office pretending to be aboveboard, while always dipping into the till for personal gain. Illinois has a long history of political scandal, so that cultural atmosphere certainly was ingrained in the fabric not just of Chicago politics but also of state-wide political machinations. However, Alex did not shrink in the face of political corruption. He called out both stupidity and hypocrisy in a public venue, since he felt betrayed. He had helped deliver the votes for Kerner's election. He knew he was neither a politician nor a mighty force in the political machine. I am sure that, to Kerner, he was a very minor player. That didn't stop Alex from giving him a dressing down publicly; and Dad was not a diplomat by any stretch of the imagination. When he needed to, he summoned the sheer force of his personality and wits to get a job done, to bring those who might have been on the other side into the fold. He was an effective amateur politico, albeit one of many in the great political wheel of Democratic politics in Illinois.

To understand Alex was also to understand the Chicago of the 1920s–1960s that was dominated by an Irish political mafia, among them the Kelly-Nash partnership. The machine controlled much of City life in those days—from garbage pickup to building inspections to construction and, of course, voting. The Aldermen and their wards were like the barons of early England, using their political fiefdoms to wield power in their neighborhoods.

> "Illinois currently [March 1940] has five dictators—Kelly, Nash, Neidelman, Schwartz and Avrey"—Lieutenant Gov. John Stelle, campaigning for the Democratic nomination for governor, charged tonight in a radio speech. "Democracy is dead when one or two or five men can say who shall be elected and the voters must vote the bosses' will or suffer dire consequences," Stelle said. While Boss Mayor Edward J. Kelly coerces the city employees in Chicago Boss [Samuel L.] Neidelman (state finance director) puts the heat on the job holders downstate. Control the ballot, intimidate the free press, muzzle the free citizens. Are these not the steps by which tyranny rises to power.[14]

What the average citizen must have faced if ever he or she had to deal with the "Machine." Food for thought for this post-Trump era we find ourselves in.

I try to understand what it must have been like to be a first-generation Italian-American in the early 20th century. Their story was not so different from those who had come before them... the Irish who could not find work back in the 1840s and 1850s when they emigrated...and those still to come. Alex's heft, spirit, determination, and grit can be found in the neighborhood and family in which he grew up, defined in

Laws don't always equal right

Call out hypocrisy

Beware of the mob mentality of fascism

Strive to learn toughness through adversity

Keep your commitments

part by a love for food, music, social gatherings, and more, and also by the City that surrounded him. Chicago in and of itself is toughness, beauty, rawness, and power rolled into one. "Come and show me another city with lifted head singing so proud to be alive and coarse and strong and cunning," in poet Carl Sandburg's words. And I see in my Dad that pride, that brashness, strength, and cunning. He was a first-genner trying to make it. While I disagreed with Alex on more than one occasion and almost came to blows on others, he gave me his joy for life, his joy in work, his joy in family and friends, despite all that life hurls towards you like a meteor. Without my knowing it, Alex gave me the gift of joy and the gift of lessons that I would use throughout my life, handing off to the next generation how to "be" in this universe.

Lesson #5—Keeping one's commitments stands out because, for my Dad, that was "the handshake," the personal promise that you would deliver on what you said. Not doing so would be a dishonor, a signal that you could not be trusted. Alex learned on his police-force days that trust in your partner was at the heart of staying alive, and trust was and is at the core of commitments.

CHAPTER 4

902 Cambridge Avenue

The Old Neighborhood

My big Italian family was part of the migration that began in the 1850s to Chicago, but it really accelerated in the late 19th to early 20th century. The Marinos were a big, gregarious family tied to old-world traditions. It was the Dominican Sisters of Sinsinawa, Wisconsin who helped those immigrants hold on to traditions while transitioning to American culture. This was the backdrop to my father's life and family.

Alex's strength and confidence, and his approach to the greater world outside his family, were rooted in his respect for the power of love—the love of family that was foundational to his ability to forge a life. It's possible to have strength and confidence without this element of love, of course; that has played out myriad times throughout history. But Alex taught me that when love is the core, the basis for your "why," it provides you with the steel to endure, to persevere, to survive, to continue. Alex taught me that love is indeed the yeast for growth in one's life. His teachings were mostly from his actions, his doing.

> *I'll be loving you always*
> *With a love that's true always*
> *When the things you've planned*
> *Need a helpin' hand*
> *I will understand always, always*
>
> *Days may not be fair always*
> *That's when I'll be there always*
> *Not for just an hour, not for just a day*
> *Not for just a year but always*[15]

can still hear this song by Irving Berlin playing in our house; I remember Alex taking Annie's hand and waltzing her to this tune.

Dad met Mom at the Aragon Ballroom, a dance hall on Chicago's North Side that had opened in 1926. These dance halls emerged as socially acceptable after Prohibition ended, and appealed to the younger crowd, especially young women.[16] Dancing was, for Alex and Ann, as necessary as breathing; they both loved to "step out." Annie was vibrant, beautiful—a lookalike of Clara Bow, one of the first silent film actresses to successfully transition to sound films, who became a symbol of the era of flapper women known for their independence and freedom of thought. Annie had a great sense of humor and a heart wrapped in kindness.

Dad stepped out of his Sicilian heritage in a variety of ways, from going to work for the Chicago Police Department, to dancing

Dad and Mom at one of their parties

at Chicago's ballrooms, to looking beyond the Italian community for women to date. The Aragon was a place where border walls came down, and Sicilian Alex was entranced with the enchanting, albeit Lithuanian, young woman he met there. For Alex, going to the Aragon meant leaving a bit of Cambridge Avenue behind to enjoy the music and post-Prohibition life. In dating my mother, he moved beyond his Cambridge Avenue roots, meeting her regularly at the Aragon and even bringing her home to meet and eventually live with his family before they were married in the early 1930s.

The Old House—902 Cambridge Ave.

Alex didn't just win over his mother, Grandma Maria, to the idea of a Lithuanian, a foreigner, in the family; he did such a good job that Grandma embraced the young Northern European, teaching her a bit of Sicilian dialect and a lot about Italian cooking. In bringing in a woman from a different culture, Dad stood up to his own culture and an indomitable matriarch! My mother's openness to learning the culture and the food helped foster that acceptance a great deal, unusual in a community where the tendency was to stick with one's own. Alex's choice of his mate in life surely showed his willingness to be not just of Sicilian heritage, but also American—yet another American "mutt mixture."

My big Italian family was part of the migration that began in the 1850s to Chicago, but it really accelerated in the late 19th to early 20th century. "They [Italians] worked in construction, factories and on the railroad around the City and others went into small trades. Before 1900, unskilled workers sometimes fell prey to *padroni*, labor agents who found work for their compatriots, often for an exorbitant fee. Women worked alongside men in the garment industry, second only to New York City, which spawned one of the largest strikes in

Chicago history led by three Italians. Success came to early entrepreneurs such as Giovanni Garibaldi and Frank Cuneo who created the largest fruit and nut wholesale business in the U.S."[17]

But Italians were always considered racially inferior to their Northern European white counterparts, and they became a symbol for anti-immigrant sentiment that resulted in the Immigration Act of 1924.

> The Immigration Act of 1924 limited the number of immigrants allowed entry into the United States through a national origins quota. The quota provided immigration visas to two percent of the total number of people of each nationality in the United States as of the 1890 national census. It completely excluded immigrants from Asia…. The new law traced the origins of the whole of the U.S. population, including natural-born citizens. The new quota calculations included large numbers of people of British descent whose families had long resided in the United States. As a result, the percentage of visas available to individuals from the British Isles and Western Europe increased, but newer immigration from other areas like Southern and Eastern Europe was limited.[18]

Having the likes of Al Capone and Black Hand members only added to the image of Sicilians being criminals and not trustworthy. "An important part of the Capone legacy is the assumption in the public mind (and among Italian Americans themselves) that every successful Italian American is somehow 'connected.'"[19]

All of this played out against a backdrop of machine political and business interests. The Irish success was a marriage between the former Irish and other immigrants from the 19th century who could not access certain jobs, redirecting their efforts to politics and government, and the Anglo power brokers of the City—Potter Palmer, Philip Danforth Armour, George Pullman, Marshall Field, and others.

Chicago was one of the most segregated cities in the U.S. in the 19th and 20th centuries (and in some ways, it still is), and not just divided by Black and white but by every ethnic group. The Italian community was not one "Little Italy" but a series of small communities based upon the village, town or city from which one emigrated re-imagined within the Chicago city limit and also in specific suburbs where immigrants could find work. So Sicilians settled in the Near North Side or Trivignesi in Melrose Park. "In 1890, the suburb [Melrose Park] was already the scene of real estate promotion among the Italians.... In 1894, the first *festa della Madonna* [to honor the recovery from illness of Emilio de Stefano] was held on the De Stefano farm in Melrose Park.... Certain districts such as Melrose Park and Kensington remain even today strongholds of Italian American communities."[20]

The ethnic barriers were real. The other half of my heritage, Lithuanians, did not cross into Italian territory, Germans stayed away from Polish neighborhoods, and on and on. Each community brought its own festivals, foods, culture, music, and associations. While my grandparents' world was the Near North side of Chicago and the 22nd Ward, life for the Marinos of Cambridge Avenue was Sicilian and American, and Alexander Francis Marino was the embodiment of striding those worlds.

Taylor Street on the near West Side was "the largest Italian colony containing about one third of the City's Italians. [My father's 22nd Ward] was known alternately as 'Little Sicily' and 'Little Hell,' the neighborhood was home to some 20,000 by 1920."[21] Most came from small towns surrounding Palermo, and at its core was the Servite church of St. Philip Benizi. It was a neighborhood characterized by honest, hard-working people as well as the likes of "street guys" like Joe "Little Caesar" Divarco, Murray "The Canal" Humphrey, and other low-level members of the Mafia, characters unavoidable if you were growing up in this area.

Our family was on the large size—ten siblings, six brothers, and four sisters under the watchful eye of Grandma Maria Azzara and Grandpa Peter Marino, both of whom I never knew. We'd all heard stories about how my grandmother would go back and forth to Sicily, with one child being born in Sicily while the rest were born in America. That one child born in Sicily spoke broken English for the rest of her life. And while my friends' relatives (Germans, Jews, Irish, etc.) came through Ellis Island, my Mediterranean crew came through New Orleans—which added a distinctly Southern vibe to our journey in America. Years later, at an Oakland A's game, I purchased a t-shirt; and the merchant, a young man in his 30s, wanted to know if Marino was my maiden name. It turned out his name also was Marino, and he was from Louisiana. When I told him that an uncle of mine was born in Thibodaux, LA, he said he was from that exact town—the long reach of Louisiana Italians!

The Marinos were a big, gregarious family tied to old-world traditions celebrating Saints' feast days through festivals like San Guiseppe, Santa Lucia, and the Feast of Maria Santimina Laurent. Saint Joseph's Day, March 19th, was for them the equivalent of the Irish St. Pat's Day, although far less visible to the greater Chicago community in the absence of a parade down State Street or Michigan Avenue.

Alexander was a product of the old neighborhood. Little Sicily or Little Hell developed in the early 1900s. The Near North Side was the welcoming center for Little Sicily's new arrivals until the Great Depression,[22] when no one had jobs. "The center of this cultural microcosm of America, this patchwork colony of different Sicilians, some wanting, some trying, to be Americans, was the Church of Saint Philip Benizi at Oak and Cambridge. Another Catholic Church, Saint Dominik at Sedgwick north of Chicago Avenue, ministered to the Irish...."[23] For Italian and other Catholic immigrants, the Church was the connector for immigrant lives, especially since the Church often included Catholic

The Marino Clan (early 1950s)

schools, both grammar (elementary) and high schools. This was a transplanted Western European tradition that followed immigrants to America. Life revolved around the Catholic Church and school, a lifeline for immigrants but also for what remained for the first and succeeding generations. It was the Dominican Sisters of Sinsinawa, Wisconsin— whom Fr. Luigi, Saint Philip's pastor, brought to the parish—who helped those immigrants hold on to traditions while transitioning to American culture. This was the backdrop to my father's life and family.

Little Sicily, St. Philip Benizi Church

Many immigrants believed that being able to work, to provide for one's family, pay the bills, put food on the table and secure a good education for your children was the realization of the hope embodied in their taking that first step on the migration road. "Work was the most important facet of life except for family. It still is: Article 1 of the Italian Constitution states: *Italy is a Republic founded on the principle of labor.*" Work equated to taking care of one's family, and family was everything for the Italians.[24] In that vein, my Uncle Jasper became head

Sicilian Feast at St. Philip's

candy maker at Andes Candy Company. He was a quiet man who never married, worked every day, and came home to meals cooked by his sister, Grace. Jasper served his country in World War I. Uncle Pete was a civil engineer and worked for Cook County government; he was handsome, a man who had seen the worst of World War II, serving at the Battle of the Bulge under General Patton. He walked around with plates in his arms and head for the rest of his life and always knew when rain and cold weather was coming because the plates would hurt more. Pete died of a heart attack in his late 50s at a Veterans Memorial Hall playing poker, holding a dead man's hand.

Little Sicily was a mélange of skilled trade workers, merchants, city workers, and the occasional mob-affiliated neighbors. It would have been unusual for anyone living in those neighborhoods not to have known some of these criminal types, but that didn't mean that your Italian DNA automatically had the "black hand" chromosome. Actually, there were Sicilians who formed the "White Hand" organization to actively work against criminal activity such as extortion. "Law-abiding leaders of the Sicilian Union in Chicago attempted to rid their organization of any identification with organized crime and improve

The Marinos at Paw Paw Lake, Michigan, 1941

the standing of Italian Americans in the larger society by changing the organization's name in 1925 to the Italo-American National Union."[25]

My Dad's journey was marked by a Depression and two wars, but his is the story of everyman, not just an Italian, a "dago," a Johnny-come lately to white America. He was lucky to have a loving, supportive family. He attended public school, learned the electrician's trade, chose to join the police force, and was able to work his way to detective. He was able to give his children a good education, with several attending college. He was able to put food on the table and a roof over his children's heads, and he enjoyed his family and friends in a close-knit community. That story, I think, has been repeated in communities and generations in many corners of this country. He was raised, along with his ten siblings, by his mother, who was assisted in this by his older brother Jasper and his brother-in-law, Vito Amaro, who married his older sister Grace. Grandpa Peter had passed away, and Grandma Maria needed help managing this brood of ten. Alex was a child of Sicily *and* America, his birthplace.

LESSON #6: Bring Fairness to the Problem— Equality Is the Gold Standard

Alex the Detective

Alexander Francis' time on the Chicago Police Department's team reflected the family's assimilation into the fabric of what was America at that time and place in Chicago. Alex joined the Chicago police force in 1938, which was no mean trick since the "Irish Mafia" wasn't exactly open to all the other "types" of city residents. Alex was married by then, with a family, so I am sure the prospect of a salary and benefits enticed him to apply. Knowing Dad's propensity to be in constant movement like a whirling dervish, plus his curiosity, these traits undoubtedly were piqued by what could certainly be, in good times, an interesting job and at the worst, never boring. The Marinos had a work ethic, for sure; and that, plus his energy level and ability to plow through distractions to solve a situation, stood him in good stead with his superiors, even if his name wasn't "O'Connor or O'Rourke."

A poem I came across in the Chicago Police Digest from April 1940 has an interesting comment on what constituted "America" from the Irish perspective. While it ends on a positive note, you can hear between the lines the lament for the loss of having only Irish on the police force and the mix of the "other" coming in (Poles, Germans, Jews, and maybe a few other Eastern Europeans thrown in, along with the occasional African American). Interestingly, there are no Italian names listed.

The Vanishing Irish

Did you ever stop and ponder
(Way back when, of course)
How the Kellys, Ryans
   and Dooleys
Were the men that ruled
   the "force"?

No matter where you wandered
In large cities of that time,
You'd meet Dugan, Shea
   and Barry,
Nelligan, Cooney, O'Brien

But times have changed in
   recent years;
Now others have their say—
The Irish hardly celebrate
Even old St. Patrick's day.

When the sergeant calls the
   roll nowadays
You hear a different chirp:
It's Wisnewski! Katz! And
   Schoenfuse!
(You seldom hear of Burke).

All you'd hear was Rohan
   and Murphy
Flannigan, Duffy and McQuin;
Now it's Mikus! Sprog!
   And Woelfel!
Pilduski! Bloom! And Vinn!

You remember Sergeant
Jerry Lynch
Who worked at Thirty-five?
And dapper Jimmy Nugent
Yes, these lads are still alive.

But they're living on
   their pensions
And their places have been filled
With Roenkranz and Spirko,
Kubiat and Schnild.

Guess it doesn't make much
   difference
If they call them Moe or James,
They're just one grand big family
And good American name![26]

Dad joined the police force and remained there until 1960. As I said, steady pay and the need to move constantly probably were some key motivating factors for joining. I don't know if Alex was ADD, but probably so, since he had incredibly high energy and stamina. He was a "type A" personality and would, I think, get bored easily. While the life of a cop was boring in some respects, it would offer a range of duties that varied daily and would have been intriguing to Alex— everything from the mundane (like completing reports) to the marvelously crazy that had him mixing with both the *hoi* polloi of Chicago to the Northshore elites.

There are many family stories handed down about my Dad, but what I remember most was his sense of fairness, and his uncanny ability to "make things work out." At my Dad's funeral, which had a cortege several miles long of folks who remembered his help, my brother was asked if he would miss his Dad. My brother answered, "Of course. But what I will miss the most is his clout!" The clout didn't come from wealth, but from his response to folks in need, or to having helped out the rich and powerful at rather embarrassing times. This ranged from helping a friend's daughter come home from a drug-induced stay in California, to discreetly picking up a very patrician wealthy Chicago business financier from a bordello. Because of both his tact and ability, Dad served often while on the police force as a bodyguard to celebrities who came to town—Robert Taylor, Barbara Stanwick, Lena Horne, and others. It didn't hurt either to have known a few low-level "outfit guys" from his work on the police force and his neighborhood. But knowing them didn't mean he was one of them.

As a beat cop, he was walking home one day in his uniform, his billy club close at hand. One of the "boys," a Mafia type, spit on the sidewalk in front of my Dad, who informed him not to do it again— that spitting, urinating, or other not-desirable actions on a public sidewalk were against a City ordinance. The same thing happened the next day, but my Dad had brought a blotter with him so that if the outfit guy spit again, he was going to make the low-life wipe it up. The outfit guy stood up, spit on the sidewalk again, and placed a stick on his shoulder and dared my Dad to knock it off. My Dad reminded him that spitting on the sidewalk was a "no-no," not aligning with City rules and regulations. So as my Dad said later, in recounting the story, "The SOB wouldn't listen—he needed a quick lesson," and Dad cracked the guy's skull with the Club. No more spitting on the sidewalk when Dad walked by.

Alex saw the immorality, often, of the law—legal doesn't always mean right. This was an eternal bone of contention between him and his brother, Larry the Lawyer. My Dad thought Prohibition would do more harm than good, and he really could not understand Larry's angst over him and his brother Pete bringing "spirits" to City Hall and the judges at Court who were supposed to be upholding the law. Dad saw the Temperance Act as wishful thinking and fighting windmills. Humans would always find a way to imbibe, and they certainly did in speakeasies all over the country. When it came to voting, Alex would write the names of political candidates on the sleeves of Aunt Grace, Aunt Mary, Uncle NoName (the one who was such a total dolt that I won't honor him with a name) to ensure that they knew who to vote for. (These relatives spoke only broken English, and would not have followed Chicago politics at all.) It's my supposition that Larry would have put a stop to that, instructing Alex to discuss the pros and cons with my aunts and uncle before sending them off.

Alex definitely was a man of his era, and his days on the Chicago Police Department mirror that perspective. They were also, for him, a continuation of the assimilation into the rank-and-file of the American worker. And Alex's elevation from beat cop to detective in a relatively short time also was testament to his facility with police work and his determination to get ahead. He was already American, this first-generation son, having been born and raised here. He just wanted to make sure that others *saw* him as American—like the Irish, who were the powerbrokers in government and politics, and the Brahmins of business.

Southern Italians, after all, had been viewed as lazy, disease-ridden, and not intelligent in the later half of the 19th century and the early 1900s. My Dad's era, coming of age from his birth in 1908 to his early 20s in 1925, was a time of anti-immigration sentiment—except for Northern Europeans, who often saw Southern Europeans as deficient. While I don't have evidentiary proof, I suspect that these views in Chicago, then, would have formed some of those feelings of being less than an American. This faded in time, I am sure, with Dad's family's move to the North Side, and his full immersion into his life around the local Catholic parish and school and neighborhood.

Alex was a uniform cop briefly, before becoming a detective. His quick rise to detective resulted from his becoming a thorn in the side of bartenders on Michigan Avenue, when he closed all the bars by 3:00 a.m. daily to meet the law. Alex had several partners when he was on the force, but the preeminent one was Frank Behrens, an Illinois State graduate, a giant of a man and a former Chicago Bruins tight end. The story goes that his hands were so big, he had to have special pistol grips made. Dad, of course, was always the well-dressed detective who looked like any other businessman walking down Michigan Avenue, carrying his pistol in the small of his back, with handcuffs and loose back-up cartridges in his pockets so as not to make creases in his suit! Alex's other partners included Francis O'Connor, Fred Allen, Nate DeFundo, and "Two Guns" Pete Glanor, an African American who carried two guns, always (thus his nickname).

Chinatown was, and still is, a very small part of Chicago, bordered by South Wentworth, South Archer, and West Cermak Road. There's a park now, Ping Tom Memorial Park, bordering the northwest side along the Chicago River. Frank and my Dad picked up criminals of Asian descent. Frank and Dad always dropped these folks at the doorstep of Chinatown, because, as Dad said, "They always handled their own, and the fate of the perps is much worse than anything we could have done." (At least, that was the rumor.)

Frank and Alex worked vice, prostitution, gambling in the CPD's First District, and they saw just about everything in their time on the force. Frank took care of the rape cases in this district, which included not only the Loop, but also police headquarters. Frank's sense of justice was akin to my Dad's. A pregnant woman was raped behind the old Chicago Theater while one of the perps held a gun on the husband. Someone saw this. Frank and Dad happened to be walking their beat near the incident, and they were able to arrest the perps. When the "arrestees" finally made it to their first court appearance, the judge couldn't understand why it had taken six weeks. Dad said that they were ill. Frank, I assume, leveled enough punches to underscore the fact that they were never to do this again, no matter what justice was handed down by the courts!

In those days of the 1940s and '50s there was a blackboard in every station, and detectives had to sign in, writing their names on the board. There was a "gentleman" in the holding pen who asked to see Dad, assuming that he was Catholic because he had seen his Italian last name on the blackboard. Dad asked what the problem was, since all the perps in the holding pen had been caught in a vice raid with prostitutes. This particular perp confessed, "I am Father So-and-So, and I will not be able to continue as a priest once my sin is known to my parishioners." So Dad worked his usual deals and had the priest released.

On another occasion (which was highly unusual, and probably happened because this particular person was "important," i.e., connected), Dad and Frank had to extend Chicago's police reach to Louisville, Kentucky to pick up the president of the Chicago Board of Trade, who had been caught in a raid with hookers at the Kentucky Derby, a bordello on the Ohio River. (Pretty tame by today's standards.) They returned home via Cincinnati, landing at Midway Airport. Dad took this gentleman to a Turkish bath to clean up and get him clean clothes. As it was really late, my Dad brought the man home to our house and put him to sleep on my mother's new rose-colored couch. (Of course, in the morning my mother was up first, and couldn't believe that some strange man was sleeping on her brand-new couch.) From that day forward, Alex never paid for suits, shirts, ties, socks, or hats. The president, extremely happy that the incident had been handled with discretion, had an account established for Dad at a clothing store in the Loop. Dad would go in and simply sign for whatever he picked out. Dad was an impeccable dresser when he needed to be; being the well-dressed and well-armed detective became his hallmark.

While I am sure that my Uncle Larry the Lawyer would have been pulling his hair out over these several incidents (and would have been right in doing so), Dad was all about solving the problem in the moment and doing what he considered right. In this case, he had been asked by the higher ups to "get the situation handled." I am not supporting taking the law into one's own hands; we are seeing enough of that in the news lately. These examples engaged me in reflecting about equal justice under the law and who gets helped—in this case, the President

Laws don't always equal right

Call out hypocrisy

Beware of the mob mentality of fascism

Strive to learn toughness through adversity

Keep your commitments

Bring fairness to the problem

of the Board of Trade because of his presumed wealth and community position and the priest because of his role as God's representative and his minor infraction in the realm of crime.

I am thinking about fairness, equal justice—still an ideal in many cases, not the reality. Many Congressional Republicans defend the participants in the January 6, 2021 attack on the Capitol as "peaceful protestors," even though some of them actually took police officers' lives. And, yet a Black woman, a nurse, who was totally innocent, was fatally shot in her own home because of no-knock laws. Would that Chicago PD of the 1940s have been so willing to get a poor man or a Black man out of that bordello if he wasn't someone of community standing or white? Dad was trying to be fair in the case with the priest, I believe (he didn't have much say about the Bordello Caper), and his way of handling the mob underling. Clearly, he wasn't exactly following the law in how he handled either. What I take from these is that "Lady Law" should be equal for everyone, not just those whom we favor, or who can do us favors, or who can get us out of trouble. This is still a work in progress. **Lesson #6—Bring Fairness to the Problem.**

LESSON #7: See the Human in the Stereotype

Alex and World War II, at Home and Abroad

Alex was exempt during World War II because of his position as a police officer and because he had two children at the time. When the Japanese bombed Pearl Harbor, Dad was given a Thompson machine gun and sent to guard the underground electrical vaults that controlled the City's power. He did not come home for days, sleeping in the hallways of buildings and cleaning up in rest rooms. On a number of occasions, he and Frank picked up German POWs who had escaped from a prisoner-of-war camp in Arizona. They were mostly kids, 16-18 years old, who had been captured at Normandy. The thinking among the POWs was that if they made it to Milwaukee or Chicago, which had large German populations, they might be safe. Dad caught two 17-year-old boys whom he and Frank nicknamed "Hans" and "Otto," took them to a restaurant, fed them, and then handed them over to the MPs. This was the same time that my Uncle Pete was overseas, fighting Germans.

Alex tended to see the human in all of us. He knew that these boys were German soldiers, but they were not, he supposed, building and running death camps in Europe, killing Jews. Granted, they took part in the German war machine, but Alex thought that for the most part they had been conscripted and were foot-soldier cogs in the Nazi military machine. He saw them as what they were—boys playing at being men in uniform. He was sure that if he had met them at St. Vith, where Uncle Pete was during the war, he would have shot them.

Given the racial climate in Chicago at that time, the utter disgust with Germany's genocide and Italy's participation in the Axis Alliance, you would think there would have been an intense hatred of veterans from both sides. And yet my brother remembers going with Uncle Pete and Uncle Nick to a small tool-and-die factory in Skokie, Illinois where they were working after the war. It was a really hot summer day and many of the workers had taken their shirts off; one, a German, had a really ugly scar on his lower back from shrapnel, almost a hole. Uncle Pete went over to him and started a conversation; it seems the man had been in the same area of Belgium where Pete had been. They talked for almost an hour, uninterruptedly, then parted with a handshake and a hug.

While Alex was guarding electrical vaults in Chicago for many weeks, my Uncle Pete was fighting under General Patton at the Battle of the Bulge in Normandy. Pete made it through the Normandy landings, hitting St. Lo and other French towns, going all the way into Belgium, before being wounded at a small town called St. Vith, a critical juncture in the Battle of the Bulge, or the Ardenne Counteroffensive, the last significant offensive campaign of the Germans.[27]

The German attack was eventually ended by General Patton's U.S. Third Army. Uncle Pete spent many months recuperating in hospitals in England, where he met Princess Elizabeth (as she was at the time). And this, from one of the first-generation sons of immigrants who came

Uncle Pete at the American Legion Hall
(probably 1950s). Wounded at the Battle of
the Bulge, he was awarded the Silver Star, the
Bronze Star, and two Purple Hearts.

Laws don't always equal right

Call out hypocrisy

Beware of the mob mentality of fascism

Strive to learn toughness through adversity

Keep your commitments

Bring fairness to the problem

See the human in the stereotype

from those Southern European nations—the ones that Henry Cabot Lodge felt carried disease and were not quite as intelligent, and would not provide the needed wherewithal to move America's economic engine forward. How many times has "not as intelligent," "lazy," and other such adjectives been applied to so many before and since—African Americans, Hispanics for many years, and more recently, newly arrived Middle Easterners—"those Muslims." How many immigrants and their descendants have moved America's needle forward without fanfare or any recognition?

Both Alex and his brother Pete saw the *human being* in the Germans they encountered—the young boys escaping a POW camp; a fellow worker who, like Pete, also had seen the Bulge. Having known German-descended neighbors and friends—having shared meals, drinks, and times together—my Dad and uncle were rational about these newly arrived Germans who had fought under the evil of Hitler.

They did not excuse them or forget what happened, but they did try to understand the humans who resided inside. This is a lesson to remember at times such as when the far right vilifies those who look different, have different names, physical features, and customs they don't understand. Lesson #7 asks us to see the human being in the stereotype, so that we are not imprisoned by our generalizations—and so that the real people, who collectively make up a given general category, aren't imprisoned in boxes of narrow perspectives.

LESSON #8: Love as the Yeast for Growth— Can Food and Love Bridge Assimilation?

Alex's Family DNA

Alex's strength and confidence, and his approach to the greater world outside his family, were rooted in his respect for the power of love— the love of family that was foundational to his ability to forge a life. It's possible to have strength and confidence without this element of love, of course; that has played out myriad times throughout history. But Alex taught me that when love is the core, the basis for your "why," it provides you with the steel to endure, to persevere, to survive, to continue. Alex taught me that love is indeed the yeast for growth in one's life. His teachings were mostly from his actions, his *doing*.

That doing was on display when he picked up Aunt Frances on cold winter nights as she returned home late on the Chicago "L" from her work at Carson, Pirie Scott, so that she would not have to have to take the connecting bus home down Lincoln Avenue. The doing also was demonstrated by his bringing home a delicious filet mignon as a special treat for dinner, or just by offering those choice words of wisdom about avoiding "cement shoes in the Chicago river."

While Alex's toughness, grit, political savvy, and sense of fairness were certainly a product of his family upbringing and what he saw displayed in full view in his hometown—whether on the police force, or on his front lawn by the local mob minions—his love for his family was formed not just by his mother and father but also by his siblings: my aunts, uncles, and cousins who would transit in and out of our house on a regular basis, in addition to those who lived in the apartment below us.

The rituals around food stand out as traditions that were indelibly imprinted with love. I saw that yeast fermenting in our family on a daily basis, and how my Dad drew upon that, even in heated arguments with his brothers and sisters—even at volatile times when voices crescendoed into a cacophony that could blow out the windows. Love was there displayed in many ways by my aunts, uncles, and cousins; but the way of *food* has stood out over time.

Aunt Grace was one of the relatives whom I associate with food. She spoke with broken English, mostly about family things, and she was enigmatic to me: we never had a real conversation about who she was as a person, what she thought of her life, her marriage to my Uncle Vito, their hopes or dreams. But her instinctive relationship to food and cooking, that I remember vividly. "Pally Jo," she would say to me, "bring me the flour. . . ."—or sugar or tomatoes, for whatever she was conjuring up in the basement of our two-flat in Chicago. And her eyes would laugh.

She had a deft way with dough, which she kneaded into life as all sorts of concoctions. Her bread today would be known as "artisan"— what was once just great, pure peasant bread. But more than anything, I can recall the smell of the bread "orphans" she saved from the big loaves she made, which simmered in butter in the frying pan, wafting through the walls and rafters of the building. She would fry the dough, set it on clean towels, and sprinkle handfuls of sugar all over them while they were still hot. How we would gobble these after school before doing homework, or on cold winter nights!

Grace was always busy picking herbs and tomatoes from our Lilliputian garden in the backyard. She would often help my Uncle Vito, who split rails for a dollar a day and paved streets for a living, make his homemade sausage. Together, they would grind pork and veal and beef with fennel and other seasonings to push the mixture through animal casings twisting into miniature logs. Vito—who stood 5' x 5', was a Fiorello LaGuardia look-alike and, like Grace, talked in pidgin English (e.g., *basaball* for baseball—he loved the Cubs)—would intermittently puff his Cuban cigars or his pipe in that basement, so that the sausage had a hint of smokiness (as well as your clothes, if you stayed long enough).

Food was life, art, history, language—it was the way to say what you felt at that moment, even if the English *is no so good*. And if everyday food was a celebration of life and comfort, then Christmas was truly heaven on earth. For then, my aunts and some uncles would spend days making every recipe known to man, and "in quantities that could feed the Sixth Army," as my Mom would say, because to them the real mortal sin was "not having enough!" The unspoken protocol was, like the Boy Scout motto, "Be Prepared"—just in case the entire Chicago Bears team showed up! We wouldn't want to be caught short if Justin Fields appeared at the door!

Rolling out of those ovens came *cucidati*, fig-shaped crescent cookies that—probably somewhere in Sicilian lore—had roots in Moorish culture; then, round chocolate cookies with liquor in the dough, with peanuts, cloves, cinnamon, cardamom, lemon juice, and more. A ritual every Christmas with my cousins was all of us at a very long, almost refectory, table at my Aunt's house on Ridge Boulevard. We would dunk the chocolate delights into a frosting of vanilla-powdered sugar all day long, which, by the end of the day, began to resemble that "I Love Lucy" scene where Lucy and Ethel are dunking chocolates

Aunt Mary, Aunt Lena, Dad, Grace, and Uncle Larry

Uncle Vito in the field contemplating planting

(albeit, on a factory conveyor belt) faster and faster. While our cookie dunking at the table was reminiscent of the scene from the Chocolate Factory, at least six aunts were in the kitchen making sauce and pasta. When the day of cookie baking and frosting ended, the house filled with more aunts and uncles and older cousins, all talking over each other, a mélange of pitches vying for attention as everyone sat down to eat. The smells of stuffed peppers, sauce, fennel, oregano, and rosemary, herbed roasted chicken, anchovies, and potatoes all blended into this warm, wonderful atmosphere that was family—the good, the bad, and the delectable!

Food was also the bridge between two worlds: the country emigrated from and the new home. While my siblings and I are second generation, my Dad's family, the first generation, stood on both sides of that bridge. Cucidati and pasta sat at the same table as my Mom's cinnamon rolls, homemade fruit pies made in late September (then frozen, thawed, and served for Christmas), roast beef, sugar cookies, caramel apples, and more. While Mom wasn't Italian, she learned to *cook* Italian. But the Marinos embraced the German potato salad of Verna, an old family friend, and the kolachky cookies from the Poles, and molasses cookies from that time the migrant Marinos had spent in Louisiana. The list goes on. This doesn't mean that all was right with the world, and that there were not still prejudices held against other "immigrants" who (outside of First Peoples—Native Americans) had been here the longest—African Americans. The new immigrants, mostly of European descent, still held great prejudice in that respect.

My old Uncle Vito was really worried about the Japanese-American family moving in next door in the late 1960s. After all, the residents of the North Side of Chicago had been primarily of European descent: Jews, Catholics, and Protestants. The melting pot was mostly a European melting pot. Having a Japanese-American family move in next door, at a time when the Asian population was miniscule and relegated to one area of Chicago, heightened my family's anxiety. Yet the Irish-descended woman—a devout Catholic who went to Mass every day; who, with her family, had lived in the two-flat next door for more than 30 years and who fit the European-descended profile—was both hurtful and crotchety. She was never kind to my older sister; she would yell at the neighborhood kids playing outside. Her yard was disheveled, and she wasn't the cleanest person in the world—all of which didn't set well with Vito, who liked a pristine lawn, a neat and tidy garden, and a clean house. Once the Japanese-American family moved into the two-flat next door that had recently been vacated by the Irish-descended lady, neatness and tidiness became the order of the day. My Uncle Vito and his newfound Japanese-American friend, an elderly grandfather, bonded over gardening and cooking. It's really hard to hate tomatoes or teriyaki chicken, or peonies in bloom on a spring day.

But sometimes the food or the garden were not enough to bridge the mass hysteria of residents towards someone who looked different. My brother doesn't remember this incident, but in my memory box, there was a cluster of chaos caused by a Black judge wanting to move into our neighborhood—not right near our two-flat but near the brick bungalows that stretched along Sacramento Street, on the opposite side of our church. I am not saying it was only a religious contingent that rallied against this house sale to "Oh my God, a Black person!" But if my memory serves me right, it was some Catholics who fought that purchase—and won. I often wondered what Jesus (the real guy)

would have said, since this was about as non-Christian as you could get. The judge was certainly more educated than many in the parish, I would suspect, and probably had the funds to purchase the home or qualify for a mortgage; but that skin color was really an impediment. No sweet potato pie or collard greens could stride across *that* bridge—a chasm we are still dealing with in the 21st century.

In terms of food in my old neighborhood, the 20th century was one of pizza, pasta, strudel, kugel, kolachky, pierogi, dim sum, pot stickers, chow mein, matzo balls, chicken soup, Reuben sandwiches, kosher corned beef, shepherd's pie, Irish soda bread, gyros, baklava . . . and so much more. The 21st century sees falafels, Persian rice, Korean barbecue, curry, shrimp biriyani, thai—food that follows its immigrants in their steps to a new life in a new world, to add to the layers of culture in America, to develop "the mongrel" (as past Japanese Prime Minister once called us) even further. Pizza has become such a part of our American life; who can say that, up the road, falafels won't vie for that ubiquitous place among Americans!

The American landscape embraces tamales, quesadillas, Tex-Mex—a food kaleidoscope, all reflective of culture, history, and what the earth provides in one corner of the world where ancestors once roamed. So it has been for centuries. Europe adapted quickly to the introduction of spices like cinnamon, cloves, sugar, Aztec cacao/chocolate, and more. The problem has been that foods usually blended faster than people. The idea of the "pure race" is a myth; we are all essentially mongrels, products of centuries of co-mingling, whether by choice or force. The fear is thinking that somehow one loses one's roots if there is a blend. But we still recognize the clove, the garlic, or the turmeric in a dish; we understand roots in food—an Italian blend in contrast to a Chinese one. While in the world of food, fusion seems to be readily accepted (or at least entertained), that's not so true concerning humans for some parts of the species.

Alex's strength came from a foundation of love, a strong work ethic, and a drive to make it in America that must have been part of the ethnic makeup in his big family. I never knew my grandparents Maria and Peter, but I heard from my relatives that they entertained a lot, enjoyed having people over, embraced their community, and worked hard to make a living. These were traditions that Alex carried

Laws don't always equal right

Call out hypocrisy

Beware of the mob mentality of fascism

Strive to learn toughness through adversity

Keep your commitments

Bring fairness to the problem

See the human in the stereotype

Love as the yeast for growth

into his own adult life. His gregariousness, laughter, energy, temper, and smarts (both street and academic, even though he thought books existed only for one reason—to help you get ahead) took root in the talent and communal table of the Marinos who had crossed the ocean to find a better life, to give their children a head start—in short, to chase that American Dream.

And here I stand, one hundred years later, looking back on the courage and strength it took to leave one's home and learn a new language and culture, while trying to retain one's background, history, food, music—and still *be* in this New World. Maybe in Alex's mind, he didn't achieve the *Grand Success* that perhaps his friends and relatives achieved. But his work ethic, his caring for his family and community, his problem solving, his street smarts, his big heart, his sense of justice, his ability to call out hypocrisy—all this combined in his everyday activities to move that American Dream forward as so many have before. He is among those unsung heroes, both the loud ones and the quiet ones, who worked to put their imprimatur on what it means to be American. If ever there was a time in our recent history, the COVID pandemic has shone a spotlight on those unsung heroes who have done the daily work of keeping this country going—from nurses to bus drivers to EMTs to grocery clerks. These are society's foot soldiers, and we forget them at our own peril.

Alex was imperfect, as we all are—often prejudiced, fighting the social changes that would begin with the 1960s—but he was someone who provided me with the boat and the oars to paddle my way into my life, with the great love that surrounded him and his siblings as expressed through food, kindness, arguments, traditions (both Italian and American), daily hard work, contributing taxes, trying to make "a go of it." **Lesson #8—Love is indeed the yeast for growth.** While one can succeed without it, I suppose, still the love of family, friends, and community provides the strength to move forward. Alex lived that daily, despite setbacks and disappointments.

CHAPTER 5

The Part of Our Part

LESSON #9: The "Other" Is *YOU*

Those Who Came Before

My Lithuanian-American Mom was forever known by my two more patrician Italian aunts as the "Polacky," or by my Uncle Vito as the "Russian" (she was neither). She was "disowned" for a time by her own Lithuanian family for marrying into an Italian one; they considered it a step down.

And then there was poor Uncle Joe, who was driven from the family—literally chased down Cambridge Avenue by my Grandfather Marino, as rumor has it—because he had committed the mortal sin of marrying a Swedish woman with red hair. Joe was never a part of the Marino clan, growing up—a loss to our family. The prejudice against the "unknown" was both internal—that is, intra: those born of European descent—and external, against all the other "unknowns" coming from the four corners of the earth to settle in Chicago. Fear of the unknown, of the "other," has been reflected in our legislation from the earliest time in U.S. history.

The United States has struggled with its sense of identity since the very beginning of the nation, trying to keep folks out who didn't pass the "Anglo" muster. This struggle has changed labels, but the question remains the same—who is an American?

Much have I seen and known; cities of men
And manners, climates, councils, governments,
Myself not least, but honour'd of them all;
And drunk delight of battle with my peers,
Far on the ringing plains of windy Troy.
I am a part of all that I have met;
Yet all experience is an arch wherethro'
Gleams that untravell'd world whose
    margin fades
Forever and forever when I move.
How dull it is to pause, to make an end,
To rust unburnish'd, not to shine in use!
As tho' to breathe were life!
          —Alfred Lord Tennyson, *Ulysses*

Dad's story is the story of a first-generation adult trying to make it, but it could be any immigrant's or first-gen's story. It is a story of the "quiet man," a symbol for me of all those immigrants and first-geners who contributed to America to make her "richer" than she would have been without their contributions. It is their contribution to work and the economy that pushed a nation forward.

But my Dad wasn't one of the famous Italian-heritage heroes—not like baseball's Joe DiMaggio or presidential medical advisor Dr. Anthony Fauci (whom we have all come to know) or physicist Enrico Fermi. He was an ordinary guy trying to make something of himself in a tough and sometimes unforgiving environment. To me, he represents those quiet contributions to a country that often go unheralded. We may be more aware of this kind of contribution since the COVID-19 crisis, which has put a spotlight on all those "silent workers"—the janitors, food-prep people, mail-delivery folks, trash collectors, farm workers—the people who do the many jobs that keep the economic engine of America going, and the many jobs that other generations who have lived here longer wouldn't even consider an option.

It's really hard to hate pizza or to attack sweet potato pie (just a few of the popular food contributions still with us from two of the disenfranchised populations). However, disliking *people* who don't seem to fit the perceived "American mold" (whatever that is) seems easier. The hatred or xenophobia encapsulating American culture today operates by extracting certain qualities and transferring them from one person or situation to make it "the many." A classic example is focusing on one abuser of food stamps and saying that *all* users of food stamps abuse the system. Yet prior to the pandemic, a substantial percentage of folks using food stamps were whites—40.2% in 2017.[28] These extrapolations then are exaggerated and exacerbated by media tools that spread false information, turning fact into fiction and fiction into fact, so that the basic benchmark—truth—becomes murky, and co-opted by extremists to present untruths as truths.

The United States has struggled with its sense of identity since the very beginning of the nation, trying to keep folks out who didn't pass the "Anglo" muster. This struggle has changed labels, but the question remains the same—*who is an American?* One only needs to read about the Trail of Tears—the forceful removal of the Cherokees from their native lands to Oklahoma—to know that, already, being a white European was the model for being an American. Native Americans were blatantly marginalized, their land confiscated and their "living quarters" limited to some of the most inhospitable sections of the country, the reservations—an odd name at best, symptomatic of the mentality of "keep them out" or "cage them up."

In researching this book, I kept bumping up against the "keep them out" guideline. When the Irish arrived in America, fleeing the post-1840s potato famine in their home country, they found signs stating, "Irish need not apply" or "Irish not welcome." So, like others before them, they found work where they could—in trades, as merchants, and in government, where they all but took over police and fire departments and political offices in major cities. But like so many before and after, as they gained a sense of belonging, some forgot the "Irish need not apply" signs and put up their own labels to keep out the foreigners who came after, or the ones who didn't fit their categories of what is acceptable. They would not be the first or the last group to do so.

My Lithuanian-American Mom, Ann Bubblis (no one ever knew how to spell her last name correctly—and neither did my mother, since her mother, an immigrant, never said!), was forever known by my two more patrician Italian aunts as the "Polacky," or by my Uncle Vito as the "Russian" (she was neither). "High Flame Annie" (as my mom was nicknamed by my brother for her amazing habit of needing to cook everything on high heat just to make sure it was cooked) was the "worker" who could lift heavy pots and wasn't afraid of getting her hands dirty, so was often called upon to cook with my uncle and aunt for big family gatherings. She was "disowned" for a time by her own Lithuanian family for marrying into an Italian one; they considered it a step down.

And then there was poor Uncle Joe (whom I only met once), who was driven from the family—literally chased down Cambridge Avenue by my Grandfather Marino, as rumor has it—because he had committed the mortal sin of marrying a Swedish woman with red hair (although there was probably another reason, since the Marinos had accepted the Lithuanian). He had a child whom we never met; Joe was never a part of the Marino clan growing up—a loss to our family. The prejudice against the "unknown" was both internal—that is, intra: those born of European descent—and external, against all the other "unknowns" coming from the four corners of the earth to settle in Chicago.

Fear of the unknown, of the "other," has been reflected in our legislation from the earliest time in U.S. history. The Immigration Act of 1924 was the culmination of many "acts" since as early as 1790. The primary targets of the 1924 Act were Asian immigrants; it sought to prevent them from "overtaking the country." Yet that act also limited immigration from Southern and Eastern Europe, and gave preferential treatment to those of British descent.

But this wasn't the first time, nor would it be the last, of trying to control immigration through legislation. Two more acts followed in 1952 and 1965. The '65 act opened US borders to more non-Europeans, decried by many (then and since) for the "browning" of America. Earlier, in 1790, the first Naturalization Act declared that only white people were eligible for naturalization. Ninety years later, in 1870, this legislation eventually added an exclusion of people of African descent.

Then there was the Chinese Exclusion Act in 1882—the first major piece of legislation to restrict immigration from China, even though the Chinese comprised a miniscule percentage of America's population at the time. As usual, a wage decline and stalling economy needed to be blamed on something or someone. "The Chinese Exclusion Act of

1882 suspended Chinese immigration for ten years and declared Chinese immigrants ineligible for naturalization."[29] This was an attempt at "racial purity." Interestingly, there had been a treaty with Japan in 1894 to allow free immigration of Japanese to the U.S.; but as those immigrants increased in number, there was growing resentment. "... on October 11, 1906, the San Francisco school board arranged for all Asian children to be placed in a segregated school."[30] Eventually, what followed was the Immigration Act of 1924, which severely restricted Asian and other immigration.

In 1909, Senator Henry Cabot Lodge proposed limiting immigration from Southern and Eastern Europe. This was followed by the Immigration Act of 1917, which further restricted Asian immigration. And not surprisingly, there was anti-immigrant sentiment following the World War I recession, because again Americans thought it was the *immigrant* stealing their jobs and making the economy worse. Southern and Eastern Europeans, mostly Catholics and Jews, were deemed sick and feeble-minded and unable to contribute to the American Dream. One popular book published in 1907 stated baldly that "immigrants from eastern and southern Europe are storming the Nordic ramparts of the United States and mongrelizing the good old American stock."[31]

In the minds of those shaping American culture and life, and in control of the machinery of government, non-Anglos were certainly suspect if not downright less intelligent and disease-ridden, and not in any way capable of contributing to the building of the American Dream. In their minds, an American was white, certainly from Northern Europe, and most certainly English, Irish, or Scottish, followed by Scandinavian, Dutch, German, Belgian, and French. It was a slippery slope to allow a Genoese Italian in (even though they had been coming as early as 1850) and, God-forbid, a Sicilian.

These "second-wave" darkies faced the label of "different." Not surprisingly, the definition of America, from its earliest inception, was a *white* America. I still slightly felt the tinge of this xenophobic brush as a second-generation kid, not that far removed from the assault on immigrants in 1924 that my grandparents and parents must have felt as both immigrants and first-generation children, respectively. When I wanted to get my ears pierced when I was about 12 or 13, at the time I thought the blowback from my mother and aunts was over the top. Why such anguish over letting me simply get my ears pierced? I remember my mother saying something like, "You wouldn't want to look like an immigrant!" The tinge of being *immigrant* still lingered in their memories—that somehow you weren't as accepted as those who had been born here, even though my aunts and mother were first-generation Americans! I wondered how much of that was because their parents were immigrants, or because they were not of the far more acceptable Northern European lineage. (In fact, my mother *was* Northern European, but from "the other side"—*Eastern* European. They were in the same boat as the Southern Europeans.)

Different seems to be the driving force in terms of immigration. Not that there aren't good reasons to monitor who enters our country. We would all agree, I think, that we don't need murderers, rapists, or terrorists entering our borders. But often, the fear of "different," the fear of the unknown, leads to exaggerations and xenophobia. Too many times, that all-too-convenient formula of extrapolating from one incident or person to "they must *all* be like this"—*how the one becomes the many*—fuels the fears towards the different.

The focus on "different" is hyper-intensified against the backdrop of whatever is going on politically and culturally in a country. If workers are struggling and the economy is on precarious ground, then it is all too easy to blame the immigrant for taking away jobs. Yet in many cases, it is the immigrant who often *takes on* jobs, any job, to put food on the table for the family—and in places where the third- or fourth-generation descendants of immigrants would not go. Case in point is the dependence of California and other state agricultural ventures on seasonal immigrant and migrant workers to provide the back-breaking labor to harvest produce.

"Different" comes in languages, culture, food, music, customs, mores, religions, and physical appearances. And any one of these can be an obstacle, let alone all of these rolled into one person or one group. Obviously, *sameness* helps to bridge some of the divide, where we can find some common ground among the foreign, the unknown, to help ameliorate what it is we don't like about "the other." *Accepting*

*My family at a cousin's wedding in the 1950s,
minus my brother Pete (I'm at the far right)*

doesn't mean that we like every aspect of every individual; we all tend to have friends who are close to our own way of "being," or who complement what we lack even if they are different from us. Family, we can't choose, that's for sure; and internecine warfare among family members is all too common, to a lesser or greater degree. Domestic violence is certainly endemic to some intra-family disparities and out-right disgust that exist.

Accepting means finding the common ground that unites us rather than divides us. It is about allowing each immigrant entry to find their path while holding onto their traditions, knowing full well that for many in the second, third, fourth, and generations to come, they will become American more than they were Sicilians, Genovese, Germans, Haitians, Puerto Ricans, Poles, Irish, and more. That transition to becoming American began in my Dad and Mom's generation, as first-generation children. They were closer to their immigrant parents' experience, holding on to the culture and mores of the immigrant while embracing America's, while I always consider myself first and foremost an American of Italian-Lithuanian descent.

My culture was influenced heavily by both the Irish pub on the corner and the Jewish delis I frequented, enjoying Reubens as much as

Irish soda bread. That coming together of culture, foods, music, and traditions from so many different countries has added to the mosaic of this work-in-progress we call America. As much as I love Italian food, I love trying dishes of other nationalities, seeing what new excitement awaits my palate. Each immigrant group adds its own perspective to this mosaic. Being different, unusual, should not be a reason for fear.

My memories of Aunt Grace baking bread in our basement on cold winter nights or in stormy springs, then frying the remnants of dough in butter and sprinkling it with sugar permeate my brain, and I can almost smell the yeast. And my memories of sharing bagels and cream cheese with lox after school, or Christmas kolachkys, always added to, rather than detracted from, my joy of food and fond reminiscence of a time long past. The memories of my Aunt Grace's basement cooking have seen me through all the "foreign lands" of work and moving across country, of prejudice against women that I encountered repeatedly in my career, and of being viewed as "not good enough" for some imperious people I met along the way. That label of "not being good enough" usually came from those climbing the corporate ladder, including a small businessman I worked for briefly when I first moved to California who told me, "You will never succeed in the work force; just go home and have some kids." This label sometimes lay closer to home, with friends of Northern European descent scoffing at the "bad food they ate" that surely must have been Sicilian, or always implying that somehow the Mafia had to be sitting at our table because, after all, we were not *real* Italians. It didn't seem to matter that I was also half-Lithuanian!

The comfort of my memories helped me to do battle in my life—from keeping my own name (unheard of in the 1970s unless you were a celebrity), to forging a career, to establishing a new life halfway across the country. I have not faced the lynch mobs of Jim Crow, nor the billy clubs of police cracking skulls, nor the terror of living in gang territory; but I have seen prejudice, fear, and hatred in my life, and the agony it produces in another human being. Being different in and of itself should not be a ruse for acts of cruelty, unjust laws, or xenophobia.

There has been, and still is, this constant tension in the U.S. between the English cultural overlay of the 17th and 18th centuries and descendants of Native Americans, African Americans, and immigrants. This cultural overlay could have easily been French or Spanish, had either of those countries succeeded in their colonization. The French lost to the British in the French and Indian War (1754-63); and the Spanish moved into Alta California, Florida, and parts South, but eventually lost their hold on these areas. The fear seems to be that immigrants *not* from Northern Europe pose a "clear and present danger" to the American way of life. The separation of children from their parents at the U.S. Southern border and the banning of Muslim immigration during the Trump administration's term of office are only the latest move in a long line of efforts to ensure that "only Anglos need apply."

The fear of the "different" permeates the American culture— the idea that if you give them an inch, they (whoever "they" are at the moment) will take a mile. American society is moving towards increased equality—from a greater acceptance of gay Americans; to women taking larger public roles in society, holding leadership positions in business, government, and education; to more Hispanics, African Americans, Middle Easterners, Jamaicans, Indians (from India) getting elected to Congress. This fear of the "different," of ever-increasing diversity, has been a vehicle for the intentional disinformation campaign that the Russians have been seeking for a long time; and they found the perfect tool in social media and in persons hungry for power at all cost.

Putin's objective has been and is to weaken America's worldwide strength and leadership role. Since he knew he could not do it by military force or economic strength, he was quite insightful and strategic in finding the unresolved earthquake fault in American culture—that is, some people's fear of losing that English or European aspect of American culture—and driving in a wedge to enlarge the fault even further.

According to the Mueller report and other sources,[32] the Russians made strategic use of Facebook to place fake news into that media platform, with bots (software applications that run automated tasks over the Internet) often standing in as real people. So if someone expressed a dislike of African Americans, for example, it appears that the Russians knew how to flame that dislike into hatred, and worse. By continuing to tell their constituents that the November 2020 election was rigged, certain elected officials appear to be enabling Putin's strategy of disinformation, even if unintentionally. A similar situation exists with these same officials claiming that the January 6, 2021 attack on the

Capitol in Washington DC was a result of an excessive police response to supposed peaceful protestors; but this is belied by the media coverage on that day, as well as by the recent testimony of police officers caught in that melee.

The disinformation campaign that is still extant in this country is de facto continuing to give agency to Putin's plan. The disinformation plan is a testament to "divide and conquer"—the oldest strategy on the books to let internal disintegration do your dirty work for you, and far cheaper than using military efforts. The disinformation strategy seeks to make those who don't look like the European (particularly the Northern European) "the other"—not American enough, not white enough, and a threat to "our way of life." Those who fan these flames of fear who know better become, by commission or omission, Putin's tools. The word "treason" is not used lightly to describe what happened when certain elected officials, for all intents and purposes, abrogated their responsibilities to the Constitution, the rule of law and democracy. Their inability to speak truth to power disenfranchises all of us.

Lesson #9—The Other Is Indeed You. A lesson indirectly taught by Alexander Francis was to forget that once upon a time, *you* were "the other"—that my grandparents Peter and Maria were the "other," not so welcomed by those already here. I am sure that Alex and his family were not reading history books or looking back to what had happened to Italians. Theirs was a mindset of looking forward, of assimilation. But like the Irish before them, they were wary of those who appeared to be more foreign, less European looking, a little different; and this wasn't just limited to race, but included gender as well. I remember a conversation with Alex one day about golf. He was talking about a golf game with his good friend Don. Don's wife, Lenore, was a great golfer. When I remarked about how talented Lenore was and how women golfers could be competitive, he responded by saying that she was "different"—meaning that she was the exception, not the rule. This was probably 1965, not 1900!

Laws don't always equal right

Call out hypocrisy

Beware of the mob mentality of fascism

Strive to learn toughness through adversity

Keep your commitments

Bring fairness to the problem

See the human in the stereotype

Love as the yeast for growth

Remember that the "other" was once you

CHAPTER 6

Pragmatism and the Power Structure

LESSON #10: Speak Truth to Power

Alex and the Church

Alex was a supreme pragmatist, and he despised stupidity. He didn't understand why just because something has been around for a while, it should be viewed as infallible, untouchable, unchangeable. He didn't believe that everything had to be relevant to the day; that was obvious from his conservatism around the cultural mores he was raised with in his Italian family. Sometimes, when he and I discussed those in power, he would often say that the aristocracy existed just because they "got there first and set the rules."

My parents' stand against a power structure certainly took place on a small scale. This was local, confined to a situation in our own church. These two examples, however, made me think about how institutions can so fully define us as human beings; and while often they bring order out of chaos in society, when they "go off track" they can do such considerable, often irreparable, harm. It made me think as well how difficult it is for people to course-correct institutions, and the enormous courage it takes to do so.

The ability to stand up and be counted—to speak truth to power—is a lesson I learned from Alexander Francis, through what he articulated in many small ways and in his life's work. There was no staff crafting his strategies. His actions did not affect the course of history; they were simply part of everyday life. And yet the lessons I learned from him about both pragmatism and power structures loomed large in my understanding of doing the right thing when it counts. I find it interesting to watch the paradox of how those with immediate power and resources often bow down to those who are corrupt, empty vessels, considering that those in power *have* the power to curtail corruption. This seems to be a recurring theme in history. The people who ignore the corruption are neither pragmatic nor do they understand real power—the power that emanates from justice. They are on the wrong side of reckoning; and historically, this is not a good place to be.

We need a fresh wind to blow away the cobwebs of power structures and politics in order for us to see clearly that—before we are Democrats or Republicans; before we are Buddhists, Catholics, Protestants, Jews or whatever religion; before we are Americans or South Africans—we are human beings. Sometimes, maybe too often, the labels we put on ourselves define us, rather than our seeing ourselves as who we are at our core.

There has been a concerted effort in the past 10 years to divide Americans into neat little geographic or political packages for the sole purpose of coalescing power for power's sake and at the expense of the common good—those elements needed to have a decent life as a citizen: a strong economy, access to an education, health supports, housing, viable transportation system and more, the basics that enable an individual or family to succeed in life. While some fight over what piece of power they can attain, as humans what we need to know is how we are to feed, clothe, and house our families, and how we are to survive on this planet that is sending distress signals, from massive now-commonplace wildfires to flash foods. The incompetence, greed, and arrogance on display by those in power remind me to some extent of Nero fiddling while Rome was burning. I can feel the ghost of Alexander Francis, the Chicago detective, his frustration mounting as the poor excuses for leadership do nothing to improve the human condition. He would probably throw these poor excuses into the clink, just to let them stew awhile until they came to their senses.

Alex was a supreme pragmatist, and he despised stupidity. He didn't understand why just because something has been around for a while, it should be viewed as infallible, untouchable, unchangeable. He didn't believe that everything had to be relevant to the day; that was obvious from his conservatism around the cultural mores he was raised with in his Italian family. Sometimes, when he and I discussed those in power, he would often say that the aristocracy existed just because they "got there first and set the rules."

Two examples from our family history spring to my mind. They spoke volumes about standing your ground and righting a wrong.

Example 1—Excommunication-Gate

Jean was a mother of three boys, divorced not solely of her choosing in the late 1950s. Her husband had been a drunk and a gambler. Jean had been left holding the bag and faced raising three rambunctious boys on her own. I don't know the personal details, but I remember from the conversation with my Dad that Jean wasn't a very strong woman. The boys had been getting into minor juvenile-delinquent antics, with the older one starting to steal hubcaps (all of which seems amusingly mild in contrast with today's level of criminality).

Alex knew Jean and her family because they were parishioners at our Catholic Church. Another of these parishioners, a man named John, fell in love with Jean, saw the struggles she was having, and wanted to marry her. The couple had tried numerous times to marry in our local church, but the Irish born-and-bred and thoroughly Catholic Monsignor H. would have none of it!

The days, weeks, and months went on, but no resolution was in sight. Something that Alex understood was that things can't all be only what's relevant for the day, and he knew that the Catholic Church had its rules and dogma touchpoints. What he couldn't abide was knowing that *wealthy* Catholics could purchase annulments even after children came into the picture, but that those without means were refused. One would have thought the Monsignor and company were in the *15th* century with this practice, not the 20th.

Jean's boys continued to get into trouble, graduating from stealing hubcaps to a couple of petty theft incidents. Jean was beside herself. Meanwhile, she and John had become closer. They tried once more to talk with the Monsignor. They were even willing to have a civil marriage by a local judge, although they both were Catholic and wanted the sacrament of marriage. Monsignor H. resoundingly gave them the Cliff notes on excommunication.

Alex understood that before long, the growing escalation in petty crime would lead Jean's boys to larger and more dangerous endeavors. So he went to see the Monsignor, striding that "Alex stride," the one you knew meant business. He found the Monsignor out in the empty field near the school building that served as his very own nine holes, puttering with his golf balls, shillelagh by his side.

"Monsignor, got a minute?"

Monsignor H. barely raised his head, annoyed that his parishioner was interrupting his concentration; he was hoping for an easy put. Alex strode forward nevertheless, and laid out the case for Jean and John's marriage, clearly noting that the boys—at least one of them, if not all—were on track to becoming skilled criminals.

But Monsignor H. was adamant: "Marrying them in the Church is grounds for excommunication. It's Catholic dogma. Only if hell freezes over would I marry them, and maybe even not then."

Frustration boiled in Alex's brain. He bristled that here were two people who wanted to get married in their Church who had not committed any sins, since it was Jean's husband who had left *her* and not the other way around. Jean and John were being penalized at the expense, potentially, of Jean's children's long-term welfare.

The Monsignor turned away from Alex and resumed his "field golf." Alex was enraged that someone like the Monsignor could block the happiness of two good people who wanted to provide a good home for three young boys.

In telling the story that night at the dinner table, Alex recalled the steps he had taken following the Monsignor's curt refusal.

"Annie, I took that stupid Monsignor by the scruff of his priestly collar and asked him, 'You need money to run this Church, right?' To which the Monsignor nodded. 'Well,' I continued, 'if you don't marry these two and soon, I'm going to turn off the juice. I know everyone, and I am going door-to-door to tell them what you are *not* doing and to forget the Sunday collection or any donations. This place will go dark!"

Monsignor H. eventually surrendered, and Jean and John received the sacrament of marriage. However, neither one was allowed communion, since—in the eyes of the Church—they were still ex-communicants.

Example 2—The Green Stamp Caper

The lesson of speaking truth to power was also encapsulated in the Green Stamp project—and this time it was my mother, Ann, who was the driving force (although Alex jumped in to help her reach the goal).

In those days, life centered around school and church, and the women were active in fundraising, cooking, and helping where they could. My mother ran the school cafeteria for 35+ years; she had to go back to work in her forties to help the family out after Alex's heart attacks (there were at least three or four that I can remember). Many of the women in our neighborhood and parish had two to five children and while most did not work, my mother did.

In many Catholic parishes in those days, the women were often the extra volunteer force who supported the school and the church with their own labor. Catholic parishes often had their own elementary schools. This was a European tradition that followed immigrants who came here for religious, political, or economic reasons—a tradition that took root in many urban areas throughout the country during the 19th and 20th centuries. This system of church and schools provided a bridge for Catholics across this continent. (It was always interesting to me that even though my husband and I grew up in very different regions—me in Chicago and him in Oakland, California—we shared a great similarity in having gone to Catholic schools with nuns who were our teachers during the 1950s and '60s.)

Early on, I saw the disparity between priests and nuns. As an 11-year-old, I always thought it was strange that the five priests who inhabited the rectory could keep their own names, that they had the first color TVs, that one had a boat (he taught us all how to water ski on Illinois and Wisconsin lakes), and that they all had a house-keeper and a cook. The priests could also dress in normal street clothes when they felt like it and were somewhat "off duty." Perhaps only five hundred yards away stood the convent, whose religious women were all dressed in habits, who could not use their own names (only saints, please!). They were crowded into monastic-like tiny rooms with almost no furniture, just the basics. At the height of the Catholic education era in the 1950s and 1960s, I believe there were 24 nuns at my parish in a relatively small square footage of the convent.

And the kicker was that they were not allowed to drive, according to Monsignor H. This meant that the women of the parish (like my mother) had to serve as chauffeurs to the nuns, who needed to run their errands—whether food shopping, getting supplies for the schools they ran, or whatever was the necessity. This put an enormous burden on many of these women, who had their own children and husbands to take care of.

Now, this was the era in Chicago when it was safe enough for children to walk to school, get on buses to do errands or go to the local public recreation center for lessons, so mothers were not driving their kids everywhere as they are today. But dealing with 24 nuns and their needs presented additional work that these women did not need.

A group of women—I think Ann was the ringleader—had just about had enough of this idiocy. They marched over to Monsignor H.'s office to discuss the issue of teaching the nuns to drive, no mere undertaking at that. Monsignor H. was aghast that anyone would think of such an idea and, being such an "open-minded" person, adamantly stated that nuns could not drive. To which Ann responded, "You tell me where in the Bible" (she wouldn't have used the word dogma!) "it says that nuns can't drive. Why, cars weren't invented until this century!" Monsignor H., in his usual condescending way, was outraged that anyone, least of all a group of women, would challenge his authority. He thought that they would never even be *able* to teach the nuns to drive; after all, women teaching other women to drive was a really bad idea, in his mind, even though they had done a great job of it during World War II. Where would they even find the money to buy a car? But they pressed their case, and eventually Monsignor H. relented and told them it was up to them.

These women proceeded to target the right kind of car first, to be followed by how to pay for it. They focused on a large station wagon, probably a Ford or a Chevy—roomy enough to transport at least six nuns at a time to do their errands. And then, being good, experienced, and effective fundraisers, they came up with the idea of paying for the station wagon with Green Stamps.

Green Stamps were a popular item at the time that could be used for future retail purchases. They were part of a rewards program administered by retail stores. You bought something and were given a certain dollar-amount of stamps as an incentive to spend more money later on. Families throughout the era had their Green Stamp booklets, empty pages into which you would paste the stamps. When you had accumulated enough of them, you could trade them in for a retail purchase. It's estimated that 80 percent of American households collected these stamps at the height of their popularity.

> The biggest locally of the many trading stamp companies were the national S & H Green Stamps and the regional Top Value. Customers typically got a set amount of stamps depending on how much they spent, then accumulated them in books and redeemed them for merchandise.... The trading stamp boom continued quite unabated through the late 1960s. During the industry's peak year of 1968, more than $900 million worth of stamps were reportedly sold.[33]

The women approached a local car dealership and talked with the manager. He probably thought their idea of buying a car with Green Stamps was a joke, but he readily agreed to it in the same way as Monsignor H. Because who would believe that one could find enough Green Stamps to purchase an automobile—and a station wagon, to boot!

These women were on a mission. They created what some might call a "marketing campaign" that could rival anything the old J. Walter Thompson advertising agency could design and promote at that time. They presented their case to the other parishioners after Masses on Sundays, sent notes home to families in newsletters, and canvassed the length and breadth of the neighborhood urging anyone purchasing anything stamp-worthy to turn their S & H Green Stamps in for "the cause"! The effort lasted a good year-and-a-half, culminating in groups of teenagers licking, sponging, and doing everything to make the bloody stamps stick on their respective booklet page during one of those very hot, humid Chicago summers. By the end of the summer, there were wheelbarrow-full books (literally, some were in a wheelbarrow) everywhere in the women's houses.

Although Ann and company came up somewhat short at the end of the summer, rumor has it that Alex and his good friend John, a 30-year-retired police veteran, reached out to the old neighborhood connections (some of the low-level outfit guys) and put the arm on them to find the necessary final stamps. One can only imagine the hold that these former Chicago detectives had over them. Miraculously, the necessary final Green Stamps appeared.

Driving the filled-up S & H booklets to the dealership was a community effort: the women enlisted their husbands, brothers, sons, and friends. The look on the face of the car-dealership manager must have been priceless when he saw a stream of cars coming in and asking where to unload this Matterhorn of booklets. He was horrified that these women had actually done this. Initially, he resisted, saying that the dealership could not possibly accept payment in this form, that it would never be authorized by the company. To which Alex, in his own inimitable way, suggested that if such were the case, he would contact his brother-in-law, a sportswriter for the *Chicago Sun-Times*, to place an article in the newspaper stating that the dealership had reneged on this deal. The article would obviously imply, "What will they do to *you* if you are purchasing a car, since they are turning down nuns!" The manager relented and said he would accept the S & H Green stamps as full payment for the car. An interesting lesson about what levers to pull when power holds the reins.

The next months were a swirl of activity from working with the nuns so that they could first learn the rules of the road and then pass the written tests. Many hours were spent on weekends and summer evenings teaching them to practice driving, parking (including parallel parking), three-point turns, and more. The women were determined that the nuns needed to be independent and take care of their own needs. In the fall of that year, one by one, the nuns passed the driving tests. Those who were too old or did not want to drive did not have to. There was now enough of a "critical mass" to handle the needs of the convent.

This particular lesson has stuck with me because it was a window into misogyny and the patriarchal control of women's lives that stretches back thousands of years and in almost every culture known across continents. It is part of what shaped my view, along with the influence of Alex's view that women could only do so much—a very traditional Italian (or ethnic) view of what a woman's place was. In this respect, Alex wasn't unlike the men of his era; but it was my mother's gravitas that helped to balance the scales, somewhat, in this specific arena.

What I saw as a grammar-school kid in the 1950s was both parents standing up to power; I saw my mother in the mix of problem-solving. But I also saw how differently men and women were treated, how there were not equal seats at the table, and how, in some ways, the nuns had such a servile role in the Church. While they may have been respected for their teaching ability (and not all were good at that, for sure), it was simultaneously interesting and gnawing to observe these social mores that kept one element of the population from truly making their own decisions. I was lucky that both Ann, who took the lead on this one, and Alex didn't think twice about taking stock, standing up and "getting it right."

My parents' stand against a power structure certainly took place on a small scale. This was local, confined to a situation in our own church. These two examples, however, made me think about how institutions can so fully define us as human beings; and while often they bring order out of chaos in society, when they "go off track" they can do such considerable, often irreparable, harm. It made me think as well how difficult it is for people to course-correct institutions, and the enormous courage it takes to do so.

An institution like the Catholic Church held great temporal power in Europe for centuries, working with and supporting kingdoms and empires in a reach for power. Good things certainly have come out of it. For example, as a product of that system, I received an excellent education at my local Benedictine high school. In my work in the nonprofit sector, I have observed some of the enormous support by the Catholic Church to low-income families, recent immigrants, and others trying to live in our modern American society.

Yet what distortion of faith was at play with those nuns who ran the Sean McDermott Magdalen laundry in Ireland, and inflicted horrors on so many women over so many years. The Magdalene laundries were run by the Catholic Church from the 18th through the 20th centuries for young girls and women of ill repute, supposedly to help them. In reality, the women became slaves who were abused psychologically and physically, many of the estimated 30,000 dying from the abuse they suffered. What distortion was at play with the pedophilia acts that ran rampant within the clergy, unchecked for years, as well as the infamous Holy Inquisition of the Catholic Church spanning the 12th to early 19th centuries. When one thinks of Protestants burning Catholic heretics to pay back the Catholic powers that burned Protestants, so much of this was a vast deviation from the teachings of Jesus, and not about understanding human beings.

But these religions do not have an exclusive on going off the rails. A similar dynamic has played out with other religious sects, such as honor killings in India and Pakistan, or the Taliban's religious and cultural mores that limit the ability of women to pursue education and restrict their ability to move about freely when outside their homes. For many religions, it always seems to be a woman's fault, and a woman who gets punished.

Yet this ability to be selective about who gets to be free to pursue their dreams is not limited to religion. Sadly, it is part and parcel of some governmental and political structures. Apartheid in South Africa was in place to keep a few people in power and wealth at the expense of everyone else. The courage of people like Nelson Mandela—in prison for 25 years, and never giving up his principles—or Malala, the Pakistani activist for female education who was shot at such a young age and faced death to stand up for justice and against those in power—is truly remarkable. I would love to meet the parents or the persons who influenced both Mandela and Malala, because somewhere along the line they learned this moral courage, this sense of justice—probably in the many just acts they saw in their own families. Quiet actions like those of Malala's father, himself an activist who started schools, speak volumes about helping human beings take charge of their lives.

Slavery in our own country is another example, an institution designed to provide free and continuous labor on plantations. I think

Laws don't always equal right

Call out hypocrisy

Beware of the mob mentality of fascism

Strive to learn toughness through adversity

Keep your commitments

Bring fairness to the problem

See the human in the stereotype

Love as the yeast for growth

Remember that the "other" was once you

Speak truth to power

about Sojourner Truth's call to action in the mid-19th century to abolish this evil. She was born into slavery and gained her freedom, yet she was probably never far removed from danger because of her outspokenness about her people being held in bondage.

Lesson #10 in the Alexander Francis' school of life—Power doesn't always equate to right, to problem solving, or to getting anything done. As the historian Lord Acton said, "Power corrupts and absolute power corrupts absolutely." The Field Golf incident with Monsignor H. wasn't corrupt in the sense of anything visible, or with landmark repercussions; but it taught me to question power, to question when something doesn't seem quite right. It was a lesson in understanding consequences, both short-term and long-term. Granted, I don't agree with the way Alex strong-armed the Monsignor, threatening to shut off the "juice" that parishes needed to pay the bills if he didn't consent to Jean and John's marriage. Nor do I believe in "the end justifies the means." However, I do know that my Dad was trying to resolve an issue for Jean's young sons, whose current and future actions he thought could lead to an unhappy life for them and unbearable pain for their mother. He was seeking a solution to this particular problem; to make it right.

PART II

Understanding
Our Collective History
to See Us All As Americans

CHAPTER 7

My Suffering, My Rights, My Governance

It is 120+ years, give or take, since my grandparents Peter and Maria stepped off that boat onto a new land—filled with fear and trepidation, I am sure, but also hope. Their children, all but one born in America, went on to contribute to the fullness of America—unsung, unnoticed, but indelibly etched into the fabric of the country. Their stories were possible because of the values—intrinsic to and living in that American Dream—that were so ably articulated and codified in this country's founding documents.

Immigrants are the great "reminders" of the promise of America. Each new wave brings its own mix of angst, fear, xenophobia, welcome, and perplexity to those who have come before. America is an ever-evolving idea and portrait, with each new wave of immigrants adding their particular palette to the construct of this place we call home. While the tug-of-war to keep America white has played out since the Immigration Act of 1790, I am often heartened by the fact that it is the immigrant who often carries the Constitution in his or her pocket.

Uncle Vito, my 5' by 5' uncle, often tended his small garden after a hard day's work, whether that was driving spikes on the Illinois Railroad for $1 daily or paving streets. His dark short hair surrounded a chubby face perched on a rotund body with almost no neck. His equally round hands were hard-worn by years of toil, turned brown from the sun, with rivers of lines drawn deep into his skin. These rough-hewn hands gently, almost caressingly, nurtured the toma-toes, basil, and green beans that came from that patch of ground in our backyard—no mean trick considering Chicago's arctic winters. I vaguely remember tales from my aunts that he "homesteaded" a patch of open land in the 1950s where Mather High School stands today, growing a rainbow of vegetables for our and our neighbors' tables. But as the City developed, that acreage went away, and his garden was a sliver of a strip alongside our two-flat.

Vito was a gentle soul with a gravelly voice, whose bark was worse than his bite. The grass in the back and front—small squares of green against the sea of brick two-flats and bungalows that became the hall-mark Chicago architecture after the great fire in 1871—was his pride and joy. As kids, my brothers and sisters and I were often told to "get off the grass" so many times. We always felt like we were entering the "King's Preserve." But we didn't pay much attention to his chastise-ment; and while he could be cantankerous about "the green," he often ended up shaking his head as we ran across and jumped on it, puffing on his cigar and chuckling.

Uncle Vito enjoying a beer

Looking back, I wonder why the grass was so very important to him. I think partly it was because Vito was a farmer at heart who had to raise a family of 10 when he married my Aunt Grace, since our Grandfather had died early. Another reason was that his railroad and street-paving work was in such direct opposition to the earth he loved so dearly. I also think it was because it was *his* land, that he owned it (albeit along with others in the family). Vito was the immigrant, the one who came with nothing, who worked every day of his life, who didn't take vacations (as if "What was *that* for???"), who paid his taxes, who took joy in the simple things—making homemade Marsala and sausages, and retreating to our basement to hide from all the Marino women to enjoy his "basaball."

I also took some lessons from my "Fiorello-like" Uncle Vito (short and wide of stature), ones of humility, great kindness, and modesty—all characteristics that were imbued within this big family, despite the bombastic arguments that would often reach a fever pitch. Vito quietly would slip my brother and sisters and me money to go buy something at Mr. Sheerin's soda fountain or Schroeder's Bakery. Uncle Vito always gave the money to us without our asking. He would be bent over his prized tomatoes in the backyard, his stubby, worn hands with rivers of lines etched in them showing us what a ripe tomato was, the right time to pick it, and why this was important for the journey that the tomato would take to become sauce.

It is 120+ years, give or take, since my grandparents Peter and Maria stepped off that boat onto a new land—filled with fear and trepidation, I am sure, but also hope. Their children, all but one born in America, went on to contribute to the fullness of America—unsung, unnoticed, but indelibly etched into the fabric of the country. Their stories were possible because of the values—intrinsic to and living in that American Dream—that were so ably articulated and codified in this country's founding documents. Alexis de Tocqueville, the French diplomat and historian, saw many flaws in this country on his visit here in 1832; but he also noted that the genius of America was not only in its individualism or its embrace of democratic values, but also in its ability to course-correct, to try to adjust—sometimes failing and sometimes succeeding.

Immigrants are the great "reminders" of the promise of America. Each new wave brings its own mix of angst, fear, xenophobia, welcome, and perplexity to those who have come before. Vito was dark-haired, dark-eyed, and more olive-skinned than his northern Italian and European counterparts. I wonder, sometimes, how he was viewed at the outset by the Americans *in situ*. His work ethic surely served him well, even if English was as foreign to him as hamburgers. Throughout his whole life, though, his world was Sicilian at home. Did that make him an "undesirable"? He worked hard, paid taxes, and raised a large family. All pluses in terms of a country's social measurement, I would think.

Congressional Speaker of the House Nancy Pelosi and the illustrious Dr. Anthony Fauci, both of Italian heritage, have been in the limelight for the past COVID years, and likely will still be covered by the press in the coming years. I wonder what Henry Cabot Lodge, the Republican politician who supported immigration restrictions through the 1920s, would say about these Southern Europeans he once thought to be disease-ridden and lacking the intellectual gravitas to move the American Dream forward. Perhaps he'd maintain his Anglos-preferred mentality even in the face of the facts and accomplishments by the aforementioned Italian duo. We will never know

What motivated my grandparents to leave Sicily and their little town of Sambuca di Sicilia to cross an ocean so long ago, I do not know. But they came to a country that permitted voice, that had rights embedded in its founding documents (however limited and constrained), which allowed them the freedom to pursue happiness in the Jeffersonian sense. Vito benefitted from that framework; and Alexander Francis, as the first generation of my Marino family, embraced that and began the assimilation of our family into becoming Americans.

Immigrants who come here are usually looking for a better life for themselves and their children, whether in terms of work, education, religious freedom, escaping political upheaval, or drug cartels—take your pick. These have been motivating factors across the millennia, and continue to be. The courage it must take to leave a familiar land, customs, and language to set out for a land of only vague description and foreign framework is surely a belief in the hope that tomorrow will be better than today.

When I hear some Americans bemoan the fact that immigrants aren't speaking English, I understand their concern that we should not become a Tower of Babel, with no common linguistic thread. Because we are a nation comprised of immigrants from so many different countries, a common language is a way of uniting us across those myriad ancestral threads. For most immigrants, their native language remains the one they speak or are most comfortable with. I remember how both my Aunt Grace and Uncle Vito always spoke "broken English" and felt more comfortable with their Sicilian dialect. Joseph Salmons, a Professor of German, and Miranda Wilkerson, Ph.D., both at the University of Wisconsin, researched how quickly immigrants learned English in 19th-century Wisconsin. They discovered that most German immigrants continued to speak their native tongue well into subsequent generations. "What this means for the learning (or non-learning) of English here is telling: after 50 or more years of living in the United States, many speakers in some communities remained monolingual," the authors wrote. "This finding provides striking counter-evidence to the claim that early immigrants learned English quickly."[34] The research of Salmons and Wilkerson further shows that today, it is the opposite—today's immigrant sees learning English as a key to success. It's important to understand that holding on to their native tongue does not make people bad or disrespectful of the country they live in. It is usually the subsequent generations who become proficient English speakers.

America, from the beginning, has been a multi-layered and -colored quilt, originally painted by the First Peoples, from Huron to Oneida to Mohawk to Cherokee to Ojibwa and more. Then came the Spanish and French, who laid claim to parts of this New World, only to be upended by England and its culture. "Even before Jamestown or the Plymouth Colony, the oldest permanent European settlement in what is now the United States was founded in September 1565 by a Spanish soldier named Pedro Menendez de Aviles in St Augustine, Florida."[35] A PBS documentary further added, "This was a melting pot of Spanish,

Africans, Germans, Irish and converted Jews, who integrated with the indigenous tribes."[36]

America's history has been a clash of cultures, traditions, and languages. America is an ever-evolving idea and portrait, with each new wave of immigrants adding their particular palette to the construct of this place we call home. While the tug-of-war to keep America white has played out since the Immigration Act of 1790, I am often heartened by the fact that it is the *immigrant* who often carries the Constitution in his or her pocket.

Such was the case in 2016 for Khizr Khan, the Gold Star parent (families of military sons or daughters who have died in the line of duty) who was vilified by Donald Trump in his campaign acceptance speech for the Republican Party. Colonel Alexander Vindman, the son of an immigrant, spoke truth to power, holding to the rule of law when he testified to Congress in 2019 about the Trump-Ukraine debacle. The Code Talkers—Navajo in World War II, and Choctaw and Cherokee in World War I—who were recruited by the U.S. Marines for their communications effort, fought for a country that had betrayed them in so many ways, because of the *promise* of America, if not the reality. Khizr Khan, a Pakistani; Alexander Vindman, a Ukrainian; and the Code Talkers, Native Americans all experienced suffering and had grievances, and yet still contributed to this country in profound ways. My Dad Alexander Francis, the son of an immigrant, and my Uncle Vito, an immigrant, were able to pursue their own dreams because of the values codified in the country's founding documents:

> We hold these truths to be self-evident, that all men are created equal, that they are endowed by their Creator with Certain unalienable rights, that among these are Life, Liberty and the pursuit of Happiness.

This is the most oft-quoted sentence from the Declaration of Independence, identifying key philosophical pillars of the embryonic democratic republic. The sentence that follows, however, holds within it a concept that was truly radical at the time of its writing:

That to secure these rights, Governments are instituted
among men, deriving their just powers from the consent of
the governed.

The "governed" *do* have the innate right to govern themselves; representatives of the people get to govern because the "governed" are authorizing that power. Although this idea had been evolving in Western Europe, incorporating it into the founding document of the United States and positioning it right after the first sentence would indicate its importance as a foundational belief of the founders. Of late, it seems that government representatives forget that they are indeed public servants, not kingmakers.

When the Founding Fathers stated that, "...we mutually pledge to each other, our Lives, our Fortunes, and our sacred Honor," they were taking on the most powerful economic and military power in the Western World at the time: Great Britain. More importantly, they were taking on (consciously or unconsciously) the mantle of the voiceless millions across centuries and countries who had tried in different ways to have a voice in how they were governed. Slaves in the Roman Empire, serfs in Europe, and peasants laboring under Chinese dynasties are just a few examples that come to mind. These were the governed voices who wanted a say in determining their future.

The documents that undergird the values of the United States rest on the hope of so many who came before. While the Founding Fathers were men of means, and while their vision of equality was, to say the least, limited, they did set in motion the levers of power to bend the long arc of history towards justice, the bending of which is front and center today. The ability of the governed to have a voice is the courage to speak truth to power. In that small corner of Chicago so many years ago, in a very limited context, I witnessed courage in my Mom and Dad. I think they didn't question the right thing to do, nor did they understand the framework in which they could exercise that power; but they lived in a country that, at least for some, meant that they did not fear reprisals of police, government, or other institutions. The excommunication incident and the Green Stamp caper (although I did not understand this at the time) were lessons in the ability to not only have a voice but also to let it be heard.

When I look at the Bill of Rights, I see in it the people from whom the values sprang and the reasons why. The Bill of Rights was an acknowledgement of the centuries of sufferings that were witness to inhumanity. The First Amendment protects freedom of speech and the press, the right to assemble and protest and ask the government to fix a wrong, and freedom of religion. That is an amazing amount of protection in one amendment. But *why* were these concepts embedded in the First Amendment? We sometimes forget that the Founding Fathers were only grandparents or great-grandparents away from their ancestral place in Europe. They were well-educated, versed in ancient and modern European history. Some may have directly known human suffering.

For centuries, in Europe as well as in other cultures, the ability to protest, for example, could be summarily met with brute force by a monarch or aristocratic nobleman to quell rebellion. A free press had grown stronger since Gutenberg's printing press expanded the dissemination of information to the masses. However, that freedom to read what you wanted or to print differing opinions had often been crushed by a ruler or the Catholic or Protestant churches, depending on who was in power at the time. The Fourth Amendment talks about protecting *citizens* from unreasonable search and seizure as well as their property. Too often, in other cultures and under other forms of government, the ruling class could seize property and people for their own purposes.

This is not to say that America has always lived up to the ideals of these principles. The institution of slavery itself enabled generations to skirt the intent of the Constitution and to pervert its ideals for the sake of preserving a way of life for a few. Yet the genius of the documents is that they codify the values of centuries of people who wanted a voice, while carefully wording the language to be organic enough to allow for the expansion of rights as the country evolves.

A friend recently told me that a neighbor and he were talking about how much the country has changed. The neighbor was worried about being accused of being a racist. He told my friend, "I'm not a racist. I married an Italian!" My friend was dumbfounded that even today, being Italian is still considered still not quite "white enough," or "Anglo enough." Would Vito today be too olive-skinned to warrant help if he needed it, or be the butt of racist slurs? I know from my own growing up that most ethnic groups were the recipients of names they might not prefer, such as "Lugans" for Lithuanians, or "Micks" for the Irish, or "Bohunks" for those from Eastern Europe. While these epithets might be used among friends as colorful banter, they were often used derogatorily. As the 1960s hit, Alex and his friends thought that people were being too sensitive about the labels, perhaps thinking that getting those labels was sort of a rite of passage to being an American. After all, as he saw it, *we* had to deal with it; the folks today are too sensitive! I don't know what Vito had to deal with directly on the job, or in a store, or what folks might have said behind his back. I don't know if he paid it little attention, just burying it. Maybe he didn't feel that prejudice. He never spoke about it.

Vito and Alex—one still living in a quasi-Sicilian world, the other in the mix of all that was American in the 1940s and '50s. I learned from them both. My grandparents carved out a life in Chicago for their ten children, and their 10 children went on to be hard-working, productive citizens who have included lawyers, PhDs, police detectives, electricians, county supervisors, and participants in World Wars I and II. The following generations have included a Marine, a navy jet pilot, teachers, nurses, accountants, and more, all contributing to the greater American mosaic—and in so doing helping to expand the vision of what it means to be American.

CHAPTER 8

The Sacred Trust

Promises Unfulfilled

LESSON #11: Face Your Fears and Your Truth

Our Collective Immigrant Experience

There is such a drive to assimilate, to become American (and for much of this country's history, that means white), that once a particular group has "made it"—has managed to consolidate some aspect of power in some arena, no matter how local—they look upon the next wave of immigrants, those coming up from behind, as somehow not entitled to try their hand at the American Dream.

The American Dream, however, has taken on sometimes a narcissistic, celebrity aspect since World War II and the rise of consumerism, coupled with increasing media messaging. This focus seems to equate the American Dream with wealth and the accumulation of things, rather than with the development of the spirit, of community, of crafting a new life. For the immigrant, that spirit and focus on development are still primary. For some Americans who have been here the longest and are perhaps long removed from their immigrant ancestors' experience, it seems that the perspective often gets fogged over with materialism and self-centeredness—a culture of "me," not of "us." The countervailing force to this materialism is, of course, America's Great Heart, which shows itself in our own time in truly compassionate acts.

When Sicilians Were Considered "Too Black" for the South and Even the North

Grandpa Peter and Grandma Maria stepped on the shores of America with few belongings in the late 1890s, having found the courage to leave the familiar for the foreign—this strange land filled with people from across the globe and a language that must have seemed harsh and guttural, compared to Italian. When I visited the small town of Sambucca, Sicily in 2018, set amidst a hillside looking down on sheep grazing, I wondered how Peter and Maria adjusted from the relative calm in the Sicilian hills, with nature everywhere, to the cacophony of noises vying for attention in New Orleans.

Peter and Maria worked hard in America, and were viewed—perhaps by those who came before, Irish and Anglos—as not being of "the right stock." In researching my own family's ancestry, I came upon the fact that many Italian immigrants came through New Orleans, not Ellis Island. After the Civil War and through the rest of the 19th century, there was a concerted effort by Southern plantation owners to recruit workers from overseas to work in their fields, having lost their free labor—slaves. Sicily in the 19th century and the better half of the 20th century was extremely poor, and its citizens didn't have many prospects for a better life. Many emigrated to North and South America, and many landed in places like Louisiana. In their book, *Bread & Respect: The Italians of Louisiana*,[37] A.V. Margavio and Jerome J. Salomone described how Italians were treated by their American bosses. Derided for their language and customs, Italians/nee Sicilians were viewed as little better than their former slaves, especially because the Sicilians had swarthier complexions than their Northern European counterparts.

The Italians in the southern states were considered non-white. Jim Crow laws were applied to them early on. In the late 1800s, 11 Italians were lynched in New Orleans. Often, "Black" was the designation given to Italians on the census form. Some darker-skinned Italians married Black persons because they were forbidden by law to marry a white person in the southern regions of this country.

My family's move from New Orleans to Chicago was in part for better economic opportunity, but also, I would posit, because the North considered even the Sicilians white. Yet Sicilians still faced prejudice from their own kind, there. Northern Italians stated publicly that Southern Italians were not Italian at all, but a different race. So Italians from the South of Italy were doubly slammed with racism in that era—from whites, and from their own Northern Italian *paisanos*.

That same prejudice followed Italians as they emigrated north to Chicago in the late 1800s. The area they eventually settled in had been called "Little Hell," so dubbed because it was literally filled with shanties, dirty shacks, dirty streets, and a nearby gas refinery that shot plumes of fire and gas fumes into the air. In a *Chicago Tribune* article of February 14, 1875, a reporter wrote:

> "LITTLE HELL," a name, by the way, borrowed from a neighborhood in Cow Cross, London. "Little Hell" is without doubt poor. Its inhabitants are not only poor but vicious, including some of the most turbulent characters in the city. Its population is mixed, consisting of Irish, Swedes, Germans, Dutch, Poles, and Italians, with a very light sprinkling of Americans.[38]

It's interesting to note that in the last quarter of the 19th century and the beginning of the 20th, these European descendants were still not considered *real* Americans. An article from May 8, 1900 in the newspaper *Inter Ocean*[39] revealed that the Scandinavians were now considered "the upper crust"; and their views of Italians became that of their own Anglo disdainers a mere 25 years earlier.

> The eastern boundary of the district is peopled largely by Scandinavians and Italians. The latter have been increasing so rapidly that the Scandinavians have become uneasy and are now seeking to change the character of the neighborhood. The Scandinavians are the property-owners and the Italians the tenants. The landlords held a meeting Sunday afternoon, at which it was agreed that the only way to rid themselves of their undesirable tenants was to raise the rent.

The article goes on to say:

The Irish have moved from the district, and there are few Celtic families there now. The Scandinavians, who have largely taken their place as land-owners, are sober, industrious people, and they believe if they can force the Italians out they can increase the value of their holdings and obliterate the evil name of the district.[39]

The Scandinavians increased the rent on the Italians 100-fold.

Note that the words "evil" and "changing the character of the neighborhood" were used to paint Italians as "undesirables." How many times since have the same phraseology and sentiments been used on other "dark-skinned" people, people of color? The Italians were darker-skinned than their Viking neighbors. While Italian life improved, with Italians buying their own homes and assimilating into the Chicago social structure, they still fought against a political machine without any leverage from their community.

My Uncle Larry, the attorney, entered into the mix of things (as you will see a few pages later in the quote from the *Chicago Tribune* article of February 15, 1940, "Citizens Fight Housing Plan; Charge Deceit"), trying to forestall the inevitable—the "eminent domaining" of their homes to build what became Cabrini Green, named for an alderman and the first American Catholic saint (Cabrini) in early 1940 Chicago.

Cabrini Green was once a model of successful public housing, but poor planning, physical deterioration, and managerial neglect, coupled with gang violence, drugs, and chronic unemployment, turned it into a national symbol of urban blight and failed housing policy. What began as the Frances Cabrini Homes with modest 2-3 stories turned into anywhere from 7-19 story towers situated between the two wealthiest neighborhoods of Lincoln Park and the Gold Coast and cut off from the community. With factories on the decline, loss of good paying jobs, a City that reduced maintenance on what were poorly built edifices in the first place, Cabrini Green became fertile ground for gang takeovers and takeover they did with violence and crime escalating.[40]

Little Sicily had been home to an Italian community since the turn of the 19th century. It was more than a collection of houses; for those who lived there, it was their home and a tie to their ancestral farms and villages. The Italians who came to Chicago were mostly small farmers (*contadini*) from both the North and South of Italy. They practiced *campanilismo* (allegiance to their town of origin), and usually congregated with those from the same village. I saw the remains of that small farmer in my Uncle Vito, who loved the earth and the tomatoes and basil he grew from it. These little "villages" of Italians were considered to be slums by the middle class, as "projects" by social workers to elevate their status, and as another source of votes by politicians. The Italians worked primarily on the railroads, in construction, as shoemakers, peddlers, and barbers, and in the needle trade. My Aunt Mary and Aunt Grace worked as seamstresses their entire lives; they (mostly Grace, who lived in the flat below us) were the "menders" in our household.

> The Italian communities of Chicago were enriched by a phenomenon all too rare in their towns of origin—voluntary associations. By the 1920s in addition to the paesani-based mutual benefit societies, the Italians in Chicago had church and school-oriented clubs and sodalities that worked at fundraising, as well as special-interest organizations sponsored by the settlement houses. According to historian Humbert Nelli, the general prosperity had nearly completed the Italians' social mobility by 1929.[41]

Life in these small Italian villages in Chicago centered around feast days of saints, with the communities honoring traditions from another time and place in their home countries. It was a time to gather with family and friends, and share stories and foods.

> Hundreds of organizations from mutual-aid societies and sports clubs to business groups and regional associations helped Italian Americans maintain strong cultural ties. The love of opera cut across class lines and many Italian Americans grew up listening to the great voices of a bygone era like Enrico Caruso, Luisa Tetrazzini and Chicago's Vivian Della Chiesa, who made her debut in the Chicago Opera in 1936.[42]

While we lived in a neighborhood with an Irish pub on the corner, Mr. D's, and we all were "Irish" on Friday nights, I still remember as a young child going occasionally to St. Joseph Day celebrations on March 19th. The tables were filled with Italian treats—from pastas and sausages, to all kinds of breads, to cannolis—those ricotta-filled tubes with mini-chocolate chips and dried fruit. (I never liked the fruit but I loved the chocolate chips!) And although St. Joseph Day wasn't really something that my parents celebrated (mostly, we feasted St. Paddy!), I do remember the "old ones," as my brother Pete called them, still making warm bread, cookies, and some cannoli in celebration of that honored Saint Joe of their history.

In researching Chicago Italian traditions, I came across a note about the Our Lady of the Angels fire on December 1, 1958.[43] I was 11 years old when it happened, and I hadn't really thought about this tragedy in over 50 years until now. I still remember the horror that swept through the city and the Catholic community at the time. The fire burned a Catholic grammar school in a largely Italian-American community on the West Side, killing 92 children and three nuns. While the unhappy event did have the effect of improving fire-safety standards for schools across this entire country, it also catalyzed a dispersal of families out of that neighborhood, bringing to an end the City's last remaining Italian village in the decades that followed.

The same note also talked about the dearth of Italian Americans in politics in the early to mid-20th century. In particular, two figures— Vito Marzullo, an ally of Mayor Richard Daley, and Congressman Frank Annunzio, who was in office for 28 years—were named. Annunzio was quite a character (according to a *New York Times* article from April 17, 2001 by Irvin Molotsky), screaming at then-chairman of the Federal Reserve Board Chairman Arthur F. Burns that he was guilty of redlining, and specifically of redlining Italy. Interesting how that handy tool of banks, redlining (i.e., refusing a loan or insurance to those who live in an area deemed to be a poor financial risk), helps to keep "those others" out.

In the early 1970s, my then-young brother-in-law asked my husband and me if there might be a summer internship at the U.S. Capitol, since he was studying urban policy in college. My Uncle Larry knew Congressman Annunzio, who was still in office at that time. I asked my

Dad, who asked Uncle Larry if there were any such potential openings. Uncle Larry called the Congressman—and sure enough, there was. The connections to the old neighborhood ran deep.

This place, this Little Sicily, was where both immigrant Italians and first-generation Italians grew up. It was home, not just a place on a zoning map. The seizure of their homes for eminent domain was the final dissolution of their community. As the *Chicago Tribune* reported on February 15, 1940, in an article titled, "Citizens Fight Housing Plan; Charge Deceit":

> "One neighborhood may be known as Little Hell or Black Hollow to the federal housing authorities, but it is home to us and we want to stay there."
>
> That was the sentiment yesterday of a committee representing 160 property owners and residents of the near north side area which the Chicago Housing authority seeks to acquire for its latest housing project, to be financed by the federal government. The committee appeared before Ald. Arthur G. Lindell (9th), chairman of the city council housing committee, to protest the housing authority's proposal. The members accused the authority's agents of deception and unfair tactics.
>
> **Action to Be Deferred**
>
> Later Ald. Lindell and council leaders conferred with Mayor Kelly. The mayor then announced that council action on the proposed project probably will be deferred several weeks to give the property owners time to develop some other plans for neighborhood improvement.
>
> The Chicago Housing authority plans to build the $10,002,271 project in an area bounded by Larrabee, Division, and Sedgwick streets and a line one-half block north of Chicago Avenue.
>
> Attorney *Lawrence Marino* [my uncle Larry], 902 Cambridge Avenue, one of the spokesmen for the protest committee, said:
>
> "Some of the men sent to appraise our property pose as GO-men [Government Men, I presume]. Some of the men told our people their neighbors had already agreed to sell their property when their neighbors hadn't."

Charges They're Kept in Dark.

"We have asked the housing authority for some idea of the price they will give for our property. That might help us in planning our own future. But we have been kept in the darkness."[44]

This report offers a window into how Italians improved their lot to become homeowners in the early 1900s. These 160 property owners lost their fight; and that loss triggered a great dispersion of Italians into the North Side, where my family landed (in West Rogers Park), and other areas of Chicago.

Like their fellow Italians and other immigrants, my grandparents and their 10 offspring faced prejudice. But they worked hard to achieve acceptance for who they were as human beings in spite of the roadblocks placed in their way—whether that was the Irish in Chicago, who openly stated that they "didn't need no more dagos" on the police force, or losing the battle for their homes to eminent domain.

My father, however, did benefit from both his connection to the City and the rich and the powerful whom he had met during his time on the police force. These had enabled Alex to bring contracts into the electrical business of his brothers Pete and Nick—ranging, for example, from Armanetti Liquors, to the Chicago Board of Trade, to the Downtown Parking Station in the Loop. The Marinos did prevail, despite the obstacles. Assimilation happened in my Dad's generation—the first generation.

This story has been repeated for numerous other immigrant groups. However, that doesn't mean that the upward climb has been easy, or that there haven't been horrific injustices perpetrated on others because of their ethnicities.

The Earliest Americans and Their Struggles for Full Inclusion

The focus on immigration led me to look at two sets of Americans who have been here the longest: Native Americans and African Americans. I wondered why it has been so difficult for them to add their pieces to the larger American mosaic to tell the whole story.

Native Americans have been here for over 11,000 years having migrated from the Siberian Land Bridge, which was in existence during the Ice Age. Over many centuries additional waves of immigration from Asia and South America occurred. With the arrival of Europeans in the 15th century, the Native American way of life was threatened and over the next four centuries began to disappear. Europeans brought in farming, horses and home-steads and came diseases such as chicken pox and measles. Only 1.4% of the U.S. population today is Native American.[45]

Native American communities have been relegated to reservations and regulated by the Bureau of Indian Affairs (an oxymoron if there ever was one), and have had limited access to economic and educational success in this country. The tale of their lives in North America during and post-European colonization has been one of broken treaties and broken promises, even though there had been initial attempts on the part of tribes to work with their conquerors. Yet Native Americans have succeeded in developing businesses, from architecture to construction to environmental management to electrical contracting, and more. Far beyond only the stereotypical casino business, Native Americans have branched out into almost every aspect of American business, academic, health, and other fields.

For **African Americans**, their tragedy began with the slave trade, which was supported at the time by colonial powers across the world—the French, English, and Spanish, in our country—that permeated centuries of life in North and South America, the Caribbean, Africa, and elsewhere. Not that slavery was a new invention. It has existed for millennia in every country and culture, and it took centuries for humanity to recognize it as inhuman (something still being contested in some parts of the world today, such as India, China, Uzbekistan and Pakistan,[46] in the form of child slavery or forced labor).

African Americans' history is frightful and terrorizing. And yet out of their bondage, they have reclaimed their heritage and humanity in distinct ways, including in education, politics, literature, music, art, and more. Some ground was gained in the 19th century by those slaves who were freed by their masters—a few here and there. Some 452 slaves were freed under Robert Carter III's Deed of Gift, which took more than thirty years to complete. The success of African Americans can be found in such tangible examples as the founding of the historically Black colleges and teaching and medical institutions such as Meharry Medical College, to limited Black representation in Congress for a brief time after the Civil War that has increased exponentially in the past 50 years. In other ways, the unrecognized triumph of African Americans' keeping families together through the Reconstruction Era and beyond is a testament to the indomitable will to live a life of quality, not just of survival.

But the South's sheer control of economic and political power enabled those who were freed from slavery by the 1863 Emancipation Proclamation to be held in chains for another 150 years—initially through the "black codes," eventually through Jim Crow laws and subsequent prevailing prejudices in all corners of our country. While the Fourth Amendment protects most Americans from search and seizure, for those considered "the others" (African Americans, Native Americans), that protection was often ignored based on fake charges. Ku Klux Klan vigilantism was rampant for decades, even into the early 1980s. The emergence of white supremacists today has its roots in the hatred and bigotry of both the old and recent past.

What is it that makes these particular Americans so anathema to so many who hold them in contempt—if not in word, then in deed? There have been decades of redlining[47] in the housing markets everywhere, including the West Coast; decades of banks not lending for Black-owned or Native-American-owned business ventures; decades of forced schooling for Native American children to forget their ancestral tongues and only speak English. The "anathema list" is long.

The human spirit, though, adapts to survive. Even though African Americans adopted Christianity, were given Anglo names, and were essentially robbed of any aspect of their "Africanism," they kept what they could through the generations while also continuing customs like "jumping the broom" to get married, as a way to adapt, to cope, out of the sheer need to survive in those slave days.

> The broom in Asante and other *Akan* cultures also held spiritual value and symbolized sweeping away past wrongs or removing evil spirits. This is where the broom comes into play regarding marriage. Brooms were (are) waved over the heads of marrying couples to ward off spirits. The couple would often but not

always jump over the broom at the end of the ceremony. Jumping over the broom symbolized the wife's commitment or willingness to clean the courtyard of the new home she had joined.
Furthermore, it expressed her overall commitment to the house.
It also represented the determination of who ran the household.[48]

While "jumping the broom" ceremonies also occurred in Welsh-
Gypsy and other cultures, for enslaved Africans of the Asante Confederation in Africa it was a tradition they had brought from home, one
that also was adopted by enslaved persons of other tribes in America.
Marriage was allowed, even encouraged, by some slaveholders because
they thought it would discourage enslaved persons from trying to run
away and would make them more docile. However, other slaveholders
did not allow it. In every case, it was not officially recognized as legal.
Legal marriage, in the slaveholders' view, was unnecessary for a group
considered not human or not worthy of "institutions." As Professor
Tera Hunter of Princeton University put it:

> ...many couples did marry under slavery, but I think we under-
> stand that one of the horrors of slavery is that these marriages
> had no official recognition, that husbands and wives and children
> could all be separated at any time at the whim of an owner.[49]

Why, when the Black judge wanted to buy a home in my Chicago
neighborhood (as mentioned in Chapter 4) did all the good Christians
rally against that? As a child, I was aware of the odd juxtaposition of
belonging to a religion that professes "Love thy neighbor," but selectively applies that only to those deemed "okay." Did Christ apply
his teachings to only a few? The incident with the judge was a lesson
about how people's profession of faith is sometimes disconnected with
its application in reality.

The "Assimilation" of Native Americans and African Americans

What factors were, and are, operating in the quasi-assimilation of
Native Americans and African Americans? Coming at this question as
an amateur anthropologist and sociologist, I note both the presence of
obvious, in-your-face reasons and other more subtle, below-the-surface

elements rooted in the past but still percolating beneath the foundation of America's racial fault line.

An obvious factor is the *physical appearance* of both African Americans and Native Americans. This includes a different skin color and facial features that didn't meld as well into the Anglo ideal that seem counter to what was (maybe still is) perceived as beauty, as defined by a European culture and "look"—the blond-and-blue-eyed stereotype, despite the fact that many Europeans are brown-haired and brown-eyed.

Another factor may be the *cultural mores*. Not only did enslaved African and Native Americans look different, but also their customs, food, music, and social ways of being and living clashed with the then-accepted European view of its own alleged superiority, with its roots in an ancient history of art, music, architectural accomplishments (from the Parthenon to the Pantheon), literature, and more. In the English, Spanish, and French minds of the day, how could African or Native American ways possibly compete with the more sophisticated, refined European cultures? Perceived superiority in culture as well as religion was a lynchpin rationale for the economic and military greed-and-power land grab that had rolled across North and South America, the Caribbean lands, and elsewhere, from the 15th century on.

And yet there were some colonials who did live among the Native Americans, who tried for a peaceful co-existence. Abolitionists worked hand-in-glove with freed slaves to make the underground railroad work, transporting the enslaved to Northern states to be free. However, slavery was not confined to the Southern colonies. There also were Northerners who owned slaves, such as the Schuylers of New York, a well-known Dutch-descended family who were prominent in the development of Albany, New York, and in the Revolutionary War. Their descendants became leaders in business, industry, the arts, and government. Philip Schuyler, the patriarch of the family, owned slaves, and it is likely that his daughter Elizabeth managed some of the household slaves as she grew older. Alexander Hamilton married Elizabeth Schuyler, and it is thought that he might have owned some slaves for a while, although this is not proven. Hamilton was a member of the New York Manumission Society and a critic of slavery; Elizabeth came out later in life as a critic, as well.

Even through today, the alleged superiority of European culture—especially the dominant English culture—has remained. Some of it—such as the inheritance of British jurisprudence, the rule of law, and a common language, English (which is organic and ever-changing)—is an added value for our American culture. But for some, that need to be "anglicized" is (or at least has been) very much ingrained in our societal view. Part of the Sicilians' reason for their migration north in the late 19th and early 20th centuries was their belief that at least some Northerners viewed the Italian émigrés as white. "White" was the operative word.

This superiority complex may be a holdover from the time of 14th- and 15th-century explorations and earlier. An extension of this complex is the perspective that indigenous peoples (whether in Africa, the Caribbean, the Americas, or elsewhere) were really savages, somehow not quite human; the very epitome of "less than." A Spanish Dominican monk, Bartolome de las Casas, excoriated the Spanish conquest for its greed and genocide of indigenous people in 1542, but that fell on deaf ears. Under the Spanish occupation, natives were forced to adopt Christianity and were enslaved, often being beaten or tortured if they did not complete the task at hand. To add insult to injury, the Spanish brought with them diseases to which the Native Americans did not have immunity. Many of them died as much from disease as from enslavement. Despite admonishments from de Las Casas, the aggrandizement of Spanish conquests continued and, if anything, accelerated.

That superior philosophy is woven into this American quilt, and often has been used as a foil to dismiss charges of mistreatment, torture, killings, and land grabs over the course of our history. Case in point is the Cherokees' Trail of Tears in the early 19th century, the uprooting of an entire nation from their native lands to the "Indian Territory" of Oklahoma.

At the beginning of the 1830s, nearly 125,000 Native Americans lived on millions of acres of land in Georgia, Tennessee, Alabama, North Carolina and Florida—land their ancestors had occupied and cultivated for generations. By the end of the decade, very few natives remained anywhere in the southeastern United States.[50]

The Trail of Tears was instigated by the federal government, working with white settlers who wanted land to grow cotton and other crops. This need for land continued with the expansion of cattle ranches onto Cherokee land. While this was a policy of the early 19th-century American government, it had earlier precedents. Even George Washington in his lifetime believed that the best way to deal with this particular group of Americans—so different from the predominant white culture—was to simply "civilize" them by making them more "white."

> This could be accomplished by having Native Americans become Christian, adopt English as their language, adopt European-style economics—individual ownership of land and other properties....[51]

This massive land grab was not exclusive to the South. It also occurred in Northern areas such as Wisconsin and Illinois, which resulted in the Black Hawk War of 1832. Custer's Last Stand in the Montana territory, the Great Sioux War of 1876, was an extension of this kind of federally backed stealing. There were many other instances of this deliberate, strategic policy to free up more land for the new country by forcing Native Americans off it.

While the approaches to Native Americans and African Americans have been different, a thread that unites these two groups in their disenfranchisement is that these peoples' cultures, heritage, languages, and "looks" differ in contrast to a European template. For African Americans, there also is the added element that these former enslaved people or descendants of those enslaved "belonged" to their master: they held no lands, not even ownership of their own being. From the 17th century through the mid-20th century, that difference has been exaggerated and fanned into fear as a red herring to justify land grabs, torture, lynchings, and more.

Xenophobia—fear of the unknown or of the other, and the stereotype that emanates from it—is another subterranean thread in this American story. Though sometimes dormant, it lives in the culture nonetheless. It is this thread that Trump and his cronies highlighted and exaggerated to catalyze their political supporters. Just as U.S. Senator Henry Cabot Lodge (1850-1924) labeled Southern Europeans "disease-ridden and intellectually inferior," so whites' views of Blacks as all being "welfare queens" (abusers of federal largesse) is all too often the reason for not supporting programs like food stamps or the WIC (Women, Infants, and Children) Program. The fear that Black folk or poor folk are "stealing my tax dollar" is perceived as reason enough to strike fear as to what they might do next. "Give them an inch," the rationalization of this fearful prejudice goes, "and they will take a mile."

> ...Stereotypes highlight differences between groups, and are especially inaccurate (consisting of unlikely, extreme types) when groups are similar. Stereotypical thinking implies overreaction to information that generates or confirms a stereotype, and under-reaction to information that contradicts it....[52]

There is usually an element of truth in a stereotype—and that is what can make the exaggeration of a particular group or thing so dangerous. Yes, there *are* abusers of federal programs; we are humans, and there will always be those who don't follow the rules. (Case in point—not wearing face masks during a pandemic.) Programs such as food stamps or other federal projects are made, and used, by flawed humans. But the stereotype takes the flaw—or the perceived "criminality," "weirdness"—to the extreme. Thus, the perception, as Dominic Candeloro writes in "Chicago's Italians: Immigrants, Ethnics, Achievers, 1850-1985,"[53] that all Sicilians are "connected" (i.e., tied to the Mafia)—that they could not have succeeded, be talented, have prospered on their own without the help of the Mob.

My Sicilian-descended Dad must have felt some of this stereotyping in his early days on Cambridge Avenue—the view from the Northern European contingent that any success must surely have been because the Mob was behind it. Surely, if he *had been* really "connected," our family would all have had a much cushier, comfortable life than we had, with money to burn. My Dad knew what it meant to be judged by your last name or your background. He viewed people, for the most part, for who they were under their skins. However, he was still prejudiced in the macro, as opposed to the micro. While he saw Lou, a Black man, at our old drugstore as the "right kind of person" who was respectful and competent, I do know that he held a stereotype of Blacks from his time on the police force. He faced some of his fears and the truth, but not all.

As mentioned earlier in this chapter, Sicilians faced the double whammy of (a) white American prejudice and (b) the desire of their Northern Italian counterparts to distance themselves from their swarthier cousins. As a second-generation grandchild of immigrants, I *felt* that Northern Italian superiority and snobbery about anything that had an ancestry south of Sienna, Italy. When I was out with friends of Northern Italian heritage and we had had a not-so-great meal in an Italian restaurant, they would say, without blinking an eye or considering the effect, "Oh, that is that awful Sicilian food." Or when I was discussing a work of art from Sicily with a Northern Italian relative, they would say, "What could possibly come out of Sicily except the Mafia?" After the unification of the northern states with the Kingdom of Piedmont-Sardinia and the Kingdom of the Two Sicilies, along with the Grand Duchy of Tuscany and Parma, Italy became a unified nation for the first time in the mid-19th century. And yet there were many Italians who held the view that Sicily was not really part of Italy.

When you don't have personal familiarity with or knowledge of something or someone, this often leads to exaggeration—whether that's about how a group dresses; religious ceremonies or practices; degrees of cleanliness; the use of violence by a distinct segment of a population, such as the Mafia; familial relationships—whatever the" it" is. Too often, the exaggerations lead people to fear that because "they" don't look like me, or talk like me, or have the same traditions as I do, the "other"—the foreigner, the newly arrived immigrant, the children of immigrants, the descendants of the enslaved or First People—must all be "less than"; not contributors to society, but poachers, takers.

Another curious factor contributing to this "lock-out" in American society for African Americans and Native Americans, as well as for Hispanics and newly arrived immigrants, is the attitude of "guarding my gate"—that is, protecting "our piece of the pie" once assimilation, power, and status have been gained by the immigrant group or their descendants. Selective memory—the former immigrants forgetting that they once had been in the same shoes as those newly arrived—contributes to the idea of "the other," "not quite equal."

Not all immigrants do this; but there is such a drive to assimilate, to become American (and for much of this country's history, that means white), that once a particular group has "made it"—has managed to consolidate some aspect of power in some arena, no matter how local—they look upon the next wave of immigrants, those coming up from behind, as somehow not entitled to try *their* hand at the American Dream. So when the Irish saw signs along the Eastern seaboard, "No Irish Need Apply," once they as an ethnic group began to infiltrate business or government fields—whether Tammany Hall, the Chicago Democratic political machine, or on police forces—they did not take kindly to other immigrant groups having a piece of the pie that they had fought so hard to win from the Anglos. The signs changed from "No Irish Need Apply" to "No Dagos Need Apply." Today, it seems that banner could read, "No Muslims Need Apply." It is not my intent to generalize by saying that every white person is bad or evil, or that every immigrant, African American, or Native American is great and good. But we have to be cautious about applying the "they're all like that" label to a group.

The Fear of "Different"

The upfront, in-your-face fears of things and people unknown or different has been the war machine of the Republican party for quite a while. Trump plugged into that fear of the "other" by invoking the perceived superiority of Euro-centered culture among some Americans, as well as the frustration and resentment of poor and blue-collar whites who'd had such a raw deal from institutions (from manufacturing abandoning the U.S. for cheaper labor markets abroad, and especially from government) that they felt left behind. Most notable was Trump's Muslim Ban, with greater immigration restrictions placed on countries with large Black and brown populations. The most extreme translation by Trump of this fear of the "other" was the policy that brought about separation of children from their families at the U.S. southern border.

The resentment felt by blue-collar whites was fanned by their perception that there was institutional help for immigrants, African Americans, Hispanics, Native Americans, and other groups—everything from affirmative action to scholarships to skills training to legal aid—but not for *them*. Many viewed these groups as "Johnny come latelies," even though two of these populations—Native Americans and African Americans—had been here long before most immigrants. The resentment expressed itself, at least under the surface, as "Why *them*? Why not *me*? I lost my job. The factories closed. No one helped *me*." Trump mined this negativity, locked into it, and fanned it.

Physical differences; cultural and linguistic differences; a white superiority complex; fear of the "other," the "unknown"; philosophical views that these "different" people are really not people but subhuman; and the incredible juggernaut of colonial military and economic appetite for wealth, land, and power—all these have combined over the course of three centuries, both consciously and subconsciously, to greatly limit the American Dream for those populations who have been here the longest.

The Declaration of Independence, the Bill of Rights, and the Constitution embody the values that form the fabric of the American Dream—the right to free speech, the right to a free press, the right to protest/assemble, the right to be safe in our own homes, freedom of religion—the list goes on. For many of the early immigrants, these codified rights were some of the freedoms they were seeking. Yet for Native Americans and African Americans, the doors to these American values were, if not closed all the way, certainly harder to open than for most.

Those who sought the American Dream came for a variety of reasons—from religious freedom, to building a new life defined not by one's station in life but by one's intelligence, character, and talent. Unlike Europe (steeped in centuries of tradition, with its own caste system that did not allow much mobility from peasant to nobility), the vision of America was a place where someone could *create their own destiny*. While immigrants still come for religious freedom or to escape political chaos, war, poverty and more, the dream of designing one's own destiny remains a constant. Seeking a better life has been the engine of migration for centuries, and America has embodied that symbolism.

A Narcissistic Spin on the American Dream

The American Dream, however, has taken on sometimes a narcissistic, celebrity aspect since World War II and the rise of consumerism, coupled with increasing media messaging. This focus seems to equate the American Dream with wealth and the accumulation of things, rather than with the development of the spirit, of community, of crafting a new life. For the immigrant, that spirit and focus on development are still primary. For some Americans who have been here the longest and are perhaps long removed from their immigrant ancestors' experience, it seems that the perspective often gets fogged over with materialism and self-centeredness—a culture of "me," not of "us." The countervailing force to this materialism is, of course, America's Great Heart, which shows itself in our own time in truly compassionate acts—including volunteerism, charitable contributions across a vast array of good causes, neighbors helping neighbors in disasters and strangers lending a helping hand reaching across states and divides, myriad Go-Fund-Me pages to help businesses get started, and bringing someone back from the edge. All those firefighters and policemen who rushed into the World Trade buildings on September 11, 2001 are just one example on a national scale. I have seen this virtue of selfless aid in countless nonprofits in my home territory of the San Francisco Bay Area—from Saint Mary's Center, which helps the homeless and seniors on a daily basis, to La Clinica de la Raza, with its myriad health services for the community. This act of helping hands is repeated daily throughout this country. I believe the Dream is still here, and we cannot let it get covered over by the superficial elements that eclipse its still-beating Great Heart.

Course-Correcting the American Dream

If the genius of America is its ability to course-correct and to collectively solve problems, as de Tocqueville observed, then this is a unique time in American history to course correct the American Dream. If we are to realize the promise of America, that centuries-old search for a better life, then the promise of that Dream cannot be truly actualized until it is made real for everyone. The long shadow of slavery hangs over this land like a great weight. The genocide of Native Americans is a pall that eats away like a cancer on the body politic. Neither that shadow nor that cancer will be eradicated until the sins of our fathers are taken into account, and the doors to that "better life" are open for all.

There were barriers *consciously* put into place that derailed the Dream for Native Americans and Black Americans. These included: Jim Crow laws; voter suppression; restrictions on jobs; urban and rural economic development barriers; restricting the movement of Blacks and Native Americans into so-called better neighborhoods or lands ("better" for whom?); the fullest application of "no Blacks need apply" in so many walks of life, and limitations on federal support of Native American lives on federal reservations; and unequal justice criminalizing life in these communities. These factors collided and combined to disenfranchise both groups from "the better life"—the "pursuit of life, liberty and happiness" envisioned by the Founding Fathers: that is, Native Americans, whose ancestors had embraced this land for more than 12,000 years, and African Americans, whose forefathers stepped onto this land in 1673.

For Native Americans, one example of government limitation was the ration card authorized by Congress in 1883, which once again was trying to make Native Americans "white" by restricting their ability to hunt buffalo, a large part of their livelihood for thousands of years. This card was given to the woman head of the family:

...to draw rations of beef—and, also when available, beans, corn, flour, salt, and occasionally sugar, coffee, soap and tobacco.... An Oglala Lakota once memorably said, "They take our land, they take our hunting and then they force us to work for food that made us sick." When this ticket was issued, the Plains bison had largely been exterminated—an extirpation heavily assisted by white hunters who would slaughter bison for nothing more than the delicacy of its tongue, or merely for the pleasure of the kill. In the winter of 1884, government rations were so deficient on the Blackfoot reservation in Montana, the people suffered from malnutrition: A quarter of them died of starvation. They couldn't eat paper.[54]

This is only one small example of an ongoing, government-enforced process of transforming a whole nation into being "acceptable" by European-derived cultural standards.

The American Dream is fractured. We need to refocus this Dream not on sheer aggrandizement of personal wealth, but on the accumulation of soul and community, and on opening windows and doors to let those descendants of the enslaved and those who walked the Trail of Tears or buried their hearts at Wounded Knee inside the Dream for real.

The American Dream mosaic will reveal a fuller, more complete story when all the pieces combine and work together. We did that in World War II—everyone pulled their weight. "Victory gardens" were developed to raise needed food, and three-quarters of the produce in America at that time was raised in these gardens. Ordinary citizens developed and managed the victory gardens. Women became the work force in factories across the nation. Men went in as soldiers, like my Uncle Pete at the Battle of the Bulge. And some, like my Dad, held down the fort on local police forces. Tuskegee airmen and Native American code talkers served gallantly for a country that had not given them their due. We are better when we work together, when we see ourselves as Americans, not as the "City States" that Republicans would like us to think we are.

The American Dream re-imagined needs great leadership for its realization, but it also needs great workers to implement it, to make it happen. The best business models integrate the thinking of leaders *and* workers, because great ideas and the momentum to catalyze ideas come from everywhere.

America needs its full engines working in the 21st century in order to address the planet's exploding itself from climate change and continuing pandemics. It cannot address this without the full force of its historical innovation, talent, intellectual gravitas, energy, and determination. That will only happen when African Americans and Native Americans, as well as Hispanics and all of us, are fully integrated into this American Dream. Our Founding Fathers gave us a Sacred Trust: to realize the promise of America. It is on all of us now to get the job done

Laws don't always equal right

Call out hypocrisy

Beware of the mob mentality of fascism

Strive to learn toughness through adversity

Keep your commitments

Bring fairness to the problem

See the human in the stereotype

Love as the yeast for growth

Remember that the "other" was once you

Speak truth to power

Face your fears and your truth

Lesson #11—Face Your Fears and Your Truth—is really about remembering where we have all come from; that each of our families' ancestors were at one time or other considered "the other," the not-so-welcomed. Integrating into America was easier for those of Northern European descent, less so for those of Southern European or elsewhere lineage. They all were considered "different," with funny customs and funny lineage. But in time the naturalized immigrant, as well as the first, second, third, and subsequent generations of all these original immigrants, became American.

There is no need to be fearful of "the other." And knowing that we were all immigrants at one time should allow us to open the doors fully to those who still are seen as "the other"—African Americans and Native Americans.

CHAPTER 9

Fragments to Fulfillment

Lesson #7 Revisited—See the Human in the Stereotype—or Who Gets to Have Access to Rights?

It is easy to fall into the trap of despair and hopelessness, the belief that there is nothing we can do. When I find myself worrying that the problems in this country are overwhelming, I think about the resilience of the people in my family—my Dad, my Mom, my extended family (Vito, Grace, Frances, Lena, Uncles Pete, Jaspar, Larry, Nick, Joe, cousin Honey, Aunt Mary, and my other Aunt Mary—remember, this is an Italian family: why choose another name when the same one will do?—and so many cousins). I remember their perseverance, their ability to find humor in daily life, their joy in the simple things that made life worth living; their going for their version of the American Dream.

There are as many ways to tackle the existential threats to America today as there are creative souls with talent, strength, and wisdom to bring to bear on these threats. We face enormous challenges right now. If we are to wake up and change the American Dream into a new American reality—one that sets the course for the next millennium—then we need all hands on deck, not just the select few.

D ad and two of his partners on the police force were involved in several shootings—a couple with his long-time partner, Frank Behrens, and one with Pete Glanor, a Black cop better known as

"Two-Gun Pete" (because he always came prepared with two guns—why have just one when two can do double duty?). But before either of these partners, Dad had another, and together they cornered a perp in a basement. Dad took the lead to see if he could talk the perp out of the house without any gunfire. He assumed that his partner was behind him; but when he looked around, after coaxing the perp further out of the basement, the partner was nowhere to be found. Only after Dad put handcuffs on the soon-to-be prisoner, himself, did the other cop come back; he said he had left because he had wanted to be safe. That partner was soon gone.

Dad served with Two-Gun Pete for a number of years. Two Guns might be Black, but Dad knew that Pete had his back. And that's what Dad saw—a cop who knew his job and did it—not the color of his skin.

One of Alex's big moments as a detective was arresting "Yellow Kid Weil," a consummate con artist who supposedly had bilked a wide range of people, including Benito Mussolini (who was taken for $2 million) and a brother of Andrew Mellon. Weil "fixed horse races, bad real-estate deals, even a money-making machine—all were tools of the trade for the Kid and his associates: the Swede, the Butterine Kid, the Harmony Kid, Fats Levine, and others. *The Sting* (1973), starring Paul Newman and based largely on the story of the Yellow Kid, is entertaining, but is no match for the real deal."[55] Weil claimed to have taken money only from people who were themselves involved in illegal deals. My Dad told my brother he almost felt sorry arresting him, since Weil was much older at the time and was a con artist who claimed to con those who were alleged con men, themselves. This was my father's first arrest of Weil, but Weil's final one. Weil died at 100 years of age in 1976, in a nursing home. While Alex certainly knew that Weil's life had been one of a charlatan and con man he saw the human being. He was not excusing him (Weil spent another two years in an Atlanta prison, 1940-1942, on Dad's arrest), just seeing the human being behind the con man.

So what does seeing the human being behind the signified identity mask have to do with rights? What do we mean by *rights*? Rex Martin put it this way in his article, "The Concept of Rights":

Rights are socially established ways of acting or ways of being treated (or, alternatively, such ways as ought to be so established); more specifically, a right so understood is something that is (1) fairly determinate and that (2) can be similarly distributed on an individual basis to each and all of those who are relevantly said to be right-holders. A right is always regarded as (3) a beneficial way of acting or of being treated both for the right-holder and, more generally, for society. Thus, (4) it is or should be something socially accepted—recognized and protected in given societies, and such acceptance would be (5) deemed reasonable, even by outsiders, in that it made explanatory sense.[56]

And Nancy Flowers puts it this way in her book, *A Short History of Human Rights*:

The belief that everyone, by virtue of her or his humanity, is entitled to certain human rights is fairly new. Its roots, however, lie in earlier tradition and documents of many cultures; it took the catalyst of World War II to propel human rights onto the global stage and into the global conscience.

There is evidence in many ancient cultures, from the Hindu Vedas to Confucius' Analytics that describe people's right, duties, responsibilities and, of course, the Magna Carta and our own Declaration of Independence, but when these rights became policy, they excluded women, people of color, those that belonged to certain religious, political or economic groups.[57]

My Dad, I believe, saw the human in the human beings he encountered along the way as a police detective. Many of them did not exhibit the best side of our species; and many, like Weil, had some redeemable qualities. I wonder why some humans were not included in the "rights" side of the equation in history, while others were. I'm sure that property and money had a lot to do with that. While almost every culture has had some definition of "rights," this idea that we have rights by virtue of just being human has been slow in coming, to say the least.

The lesson of seeing the human is, in the final analysis, at the core of how we go about defining and seeking human rights, and who gets to access those rights, when, and how. I have never understood the concept of "selective human rights," as I call it—that only certain anointed groups have the right to life, liberty, and the pursuit of happiness. I remember talking to a Black activist back in the 1970s about women's rights and how that fit in with the movement. He vehemently stated, "Not till we get ours." While I understood the history and the urgency (then already almost 200+ years old) of seeing justice done for African Americans, to me it was a sword to the heart to once again see that women should stand in line and wait patiently for justice.

The Women's Movement of the 1960s and '70s was a continuation of the earlier women's movement during the mid-19th century to the early 20th century, which had emphasized the right to vote. That movement resonated with me because I saw the extent to which women in my own family had talent and skills, but tradition and social mores had put labels on them (homemaker, mother, bad automobile drivers, and more)—or at least had so permeated the culture that a woman's place was neither in the boardroom nor many other places outside the home. In the earlier women's movement, women had gradually pushed for more rights, winning the right to vote; but it really was this second wave that placed a focus on the workplace, sexuality, and family.

I remember the time my husband and I lived in Illinois, and he was in law school and I was the breadwinner. The State of Illinois allowed me to keep my own last name to pay my taxes, but wouldn't allow me to use it on my driver's license. For a woman to keep her own name caused a lot of commotion, back then. For me, it wasn't just about feminism. It was *my* name and I liked it, I wanted to keep it. But that didn't sit well with some family members, and I certainly had enough eyebrows raised in the jobs I sought. For me, it was more than hubris, ego, or being part of a movement. I held the memory of all the women in the history I had studied who were smart, talented, and yet had to hide their worth, their significance. For me, keeping my own name honored those women who contributed to history, only to be written out of it by the males who controlled the press, the governments, and the sources of income. I was thinking of the 18th-century European cultural force, Madame de Stael, whom I wrote about in my Master's thesis. She was a widow who quickly understood that if she married again in the France of her century, her power and all her money would go to her husband. And so she left France, went to Switzerland, and began a salon where artists, politicians, philosophers, and others gathered to discuss the issues of the day. She was just one of the many women strong enough to create careers, who—whether by their own choice or the circumstances imposed on them because of a husband's death—did leave a mark on history. While that struggle still goes on (witness the latest volley, as of this writing—the abortion laws in Texas, Florida, and other states), there certainly have been strides.

Dad's ability to see the human being even when he was in the midst of an arrest made me think about how many people have been left out of "human rights" because they were not seen as either human or humans who qualify (meaning they didn't own property, have enough money, had the wrong color skin, or were uneducated in the formal schooling sense). The comments about women by the 1970s Black activist I had encountered so long ago—that they should be "waiting their turn"—brought clarity that we cannot and should not demarcate human rights, like compartmentalizing tasks or drawing lots about who comes first in the search for justice. As Mme. de Stael said, "[The] search for the truth is the noblest occupation of man; its publication is a duty."[58]

All this is prologue to my thoughts on what could be done through a collective effort—of government, business, nonprofits, foundations, and individuals—to coalesce into an American mindset that opens those doors that have been closed longest for two sets of American citizens, the African Americans and Native Americans. In re-imagining the American Dream, the doors also need to open for those blue-collar workers, low-income whites left behind by the disappearance of manufacturing; for farmers, ranchers, and small-town and rural America; for other immigrants now on their own Trail of Tears.

A friend of mine visited a place in rural California where he had worked long ago as a ranch hand. The rancher had lived through the administrations of eleven presidents, and felt that not one of them had helped in any way to support the work being done in that small rural community. What does this suggest? Maybe it's time to listen to *everyone* who's been left out in the cold by the unequal applications of the American Dream.

And for clarity's sake, when I focus on African Americans and Native Americans, I am not saying that all white people are bad and don't have a right to their success. Not at all—I am one of them! Nor am I saying that everyone who is an immigrant or a descendant of a slave or Native American is wonderful, great, and good. I am just saying that we need to balance the scales.

There has been a coordinated effort to deconstruct the middle class over the past 40 years, an effort disguised as the path to better profits. When wages have remained flat for over 40 years while the cost of goods and services increased and continue to increase, it is near to impossible for the middle class to catch up. As the economist Robert Reich put it:

> Most data are prone to different interpretations, but the data on widening inequality are remarkably and disturbingly clear. The Congressional Budget Office has found that between 1979 and 2007, the onset of the Great Recession, the gap in income—after federal taxes and transfer payments—more than tripled between the top one percent of the population and everyone else. The (after-tax, after transfer) income of the top one-percent increased by 275 percent, while it increased 18 percent for the bottom quintile of the population . . . and less than 40 percent for the middle three quintiles.[59]

At the same time, the cost of goods and services just rose. Reich asserts that this concentration of wealth in the hands of a few restricts upward mobility because the middle class does not have enough income to pay for essentials.

The rise of fascism in this country cloaked in populism is not surprising.

> Fascism is on the rise again, in Europe and around the world. Halting this wave is fundamental, as history shows clearly where it ends. The very promise of the European Union, created from the ashes that resulted from the first attempt of fascism, is enshrined in Article 2 of the Treaty of Fundamental Rights:

*"human dignity, freedom, democracy, equality [...], in a society in which pluralism, non-discrimination, tolerance, justice, solidarity and equality between women and men prevail." But to and stop fascism, **we must understand where it comes from, from where it feeds**. It mixes **nationalistic and social stances**, using people's discontent with **inequality and poverty**, their desire for security, and promise simple measures to protect them.*[60]

When a great portion of the population does not feel that they share in the economic pie, that government isn't responsive to their needs, then they look for someone or something to help them get ahead, to put food on the table for their families—to even be able to raise a family. After all, this is a *representative* democracy—those politicians are there to protect the country and to aid the general welfare, and "general" is not the top 1/10th of 1%. You need only look at the post-World War I devastation in Germany, where it took literally bushels of Deutsch marks to buy a loaf of bread. The decades after that war were the breeding ground for the raw evil that became the Nazis and Hitler. It's rather salt in the wound to see that certain members of Congress fought over a $15 per hour minimum wage, when in reality, according to Robert Reich, it really should be $24 per hour. What propelled the economy post-World War II was not just innovation, but also the strength of a middle class that could afford to buy things in a consumer economy.

While the Trump administration did nothing to stem the tide of COVID and its minions spoke about how great the economy was, it was the Europeans who continued to provide *real* support in terms of 2/3rds wage support during the pandemic. Why? They understood that for an economy to come back from a blow like a pandemic, workers are needed, money needs to be circulating in the economy *during* the pandemic, and Europe need to be ready to hit the ground running when COVID is under control. They were economically more forward thinking than the pre-Biden administration.

What follows below, in "Capitalism with a Conscience," is my thinking about how to balance those scales, both specifically and with a "blue-sky" view. Some of these have been suggested long ago, while some are rather nascent. Some are mine; some belong to others;

and some, like the suggestion about Native Americans stewarding our national parks, can emerge simultaneously, as it indeed did from my own brain and also from the thinking of others. I was happy to learn about David Treuer's article, "Return the National Parks to the Tribes" in *The Atlantic*.[61] It's good to know that I am not alone in my view of what could be. Emerging from COVID, we as a nation need to see the possibilities and potential for a stronger, more unified, more creative and energetic country, one that taps into the enormous talent of ordinary people who are the engines of prosperity.

Capitalism with a Conscience

A strong middle class is a stabilizing factor in society—not just economically but also socially. The diffusion of wealth across all sectors of society, not just the top 1%, undergirds political and social stability. A stronger middle class does not negate innovation, individual worth, entrepreneurship, invention, or the accumulation of wealth. It provides the necessary yeast to grow better, stronger, and more creatively for a larger group of people than just the select few. While the United States still leads the world in the number of billionaires, the top 20 countries in 2020 ranged from China (coming in second), Germany (third), India (fourth) through to Spain—countries that still offer fertile ground for innovation.[62] Most countries have done this (China and Russia being outliers), providing a social safety net for the masses of workers who are not even close to millionaire status. For example, the Europeans—although they are not perfect and have their own issues—long ago faced down the rise of "fake news," which is fascism's stock in trade. They know first-hand the havoc it can wreak.

Out of the chaos of World War II came prosperity in the United States, and my Dad's family became even more middle class than before, bolstered by an economy that surged into high gear. While they did not live in the lap of luxury (the jobs held by the Marino siblings ranged from cop to county worker), they had food on the table, could buy a car, could occasionally take short vacations, and had enough money to buy clothes and send their kids to school. There was a stability and sense of security that permeated their daily lives as much as it could anyone's. They benefited from the fact that the U.S. industry was able to pivot from making tanks and fighter planes during wartime to appliances and houses in a very short time. Not everyone benefited equally, that's for sure; however, the 1950s saw tremendous economic growth.

"Pattie Jo," my Dad used to tell me, "whatever you do, never get mixed up with the mob. You will end up in the Chicago river with cement shoes." *That* mob, you can identify, you can see; the FBI tracks them, right? But the mob that is more difficult to identify are the architects of an economic idea gone wrong—i.e., profits at all cost. The post-World War II era saw an economy that responded to need and was planning for the long haul: that saw *reasonable profits* as the goal, not egregious profit mongering—profits at any and all cost. Be wary of getting involved with *this* mob: our collective feet will be in cement shoes that bury the vision of a rich, vibrant, many-threaded economy that works for all.

And lest you think I am *anti*-capitalism, I am not. On one hand, Pope Francis called the current capitalist system "intolerable," and "unbridled." However, on the other hand, in a World Economic Forum article, "Does Capitalism Cause Poverty?"[63] Harvard Growth Lab founder Ricardo Hausman states that capitalist employment is directly related to better living, showing data from the country of Colombia, parts of Mexico, and other underdeveloped countries where people are employed by private businesses. Pope Francis criticized the idea of profit at any price back in 2015. Somewhere between these two views, I think, is an answer.

The market economy has improved the common person's ability to improve their lot in life; but when the economy is concentrated in the hands of a few and without any democratic guardrails, it can get to look a lot like the Russian economy. As someone without an economist's training but with an amateur historian's perspective, I believe that what we need is *capitalism with a conscience*. Sheer greed does nothing for the masses, just for the few. The label of "socialism" is thrown around a lot to scare people into fearing that government will control every aspect of our personal life. But look no further than corporate America—an incredible welfare state for some (not all) companies, with amazing loopholes that have allowed a firm such as General Electric to pay no taxes for many years, or that have allowed former President Trump to pay only $750.00 on a multi-million-dollar enterprise one year. Something is amiss.

Franklin Delano Roosevelt's social safety net of Social Security and the 1965 Medicare legislation has been credited with keeping people out of poverty, and the polls indicate that the majority of people in the U.S. would not want that taken away. There is recent research that Americans view health care in the same vein as Social Security—a right or a benefit that should be available to all. Medicaid, one aspect of health care, demonstrates this. An article in *The Commonwealth Fund* reveals that:

> In states that have not yet expanded, three-quarters of likely voters favor **expansion**—including two-thirds of independents and nearly half of Republicans. Swing states that have expanded Medicaid have seen better health outcomes and more....[64]

The Affordable Care Act, better known as Obamacare, is a first step towards that thinking of expanding health-care benefits. Again, polls have indicated that Americans think getting sick should not mean the loss of a home, business bankruptcies, savings depletions, and more. It seems to me that we can be capitalists and still bring others into the fold and share the benefits of the system—like walking and chewing gum at the same time!

While my Dad probably would have scoffed at some of these ideas and maybe been incensed by others (such as reparations), *he* probably could have used some help, such as forgivable loans, to help keep his brothers' electrical contractor's business afloat while he convalesced with angina and multiple heart attacks. Alex would have bristled at what he might have viewed as "hand-outs"; but in light of the cancer and heart issues that affected family members—and the corresponding drug costs they must have incurred—I'm sure that some support to reduce costs would have been welcomed. I believe that my grandparents did not come to this country looking for a handout, but rather a hand up. If there had been more available resources for college attendance, I wonder if some of their offspring would have gone.

The ideas presented here are simply food for thought. How can we, as a nation, be the rising tide that lifts all boats—and not just in America, but worldwide? We are, after all, global citizens who share a common planet that desperately needs our help *now*, not 20 years from now. If during WWII we had taken forever to pivot to turn commercial factories into war-time manufacturers of planes, guns, and more, then Europe and America would surely have lost the war to the Nazis. It's time to pivot, to do that ingenious thing that's so very American—course correct (as de Tocqueville observed) and bring along our fellow countrymen and women who have been left out in the cold.

This is a threshold moment in American history, a moment that calls for the bold, innovative, and upending thinking that is so classically US! It is a time to stretch the imagination to meet the need. "Make no little plans," as architect Daniel Burnham said for rebuilding the City after the Chicago fire in 1871:

> Make no little plans. They have no magic to stir men's blood and probably themselves will not be realized. Make big plans; aim high in hope and work, remembering that a noble, logical diagram once recorded will never die, but long after we are gone will be a living thing, asserting itself with ever-growing insistency. Remember that our sons and grandsons are going to do things that would stagger us. Let your watchword be order and your beacon beauty. Think big.[65]

This is not a time in our history for "small thoughts!"

Thinking Big—Recommendations on Balancing the Scale

In this section, I offer my own recommendations on what could be done to right the wrongs alluded to in this book. I know full well that they are "just" ideas, that ideas are easy to come up with, and that the real work lies in developing plans for implementation—the trench work that will surely have to be done around any ideas that percolate from our collective American mind. Still, every step in the direction of true democracy, including the work of the Founding Fathers, starts with an idea and an ideal, and a dedication to taking that step. And so the recommendations that follow reflect those lessons that I learned so long ago from my father and have explored in depth in this book:

- *Laws do not always equal right*
- *Call out hypocrisy*
- *Beware of the mob mentality of fascism*

- *Keep your commitments*
- *Solve the problem*
- *See the human in the stereotype*
- *Remember that the "other" was once you*
- *Love as the yeast for growth*
- *Face our fears and our truth.*

To right this ship we call the American Dream, we need an honest, forthright, problem-solving, human, and fearless approach. We need to face the truth of the past so that we can have a future that is free for all—to be free to purchase a house where you want; free to be judged by your talents, integrity and ethics, not by your skin color or stereotype; free to have access to equal justice under the law; free to go for a jog and not get shot. Love is what enables the resurrection of this Dream—the ability to finally make those vital American documents (including the Declaration of Independence and the Constitution) fulfill their promise.

My recommendations below suggest just a few possibilities of "what might be." While you may or may not agree with them, you can view them as a springboard to brainstorming and developing real pathways to equality, justice, and just plain better living for us all. I offer these suggestions as a catalyst for larger discussions and the formulation of next steps.

In Chapter 11, "Lessons from America: Reflections on Adding Your Pieces to the American Mosaic," I will be asking you for *your* thoughts, *your* ideas, *your* feedback—the best of your gray matter on any and all of these ideas. Once you have formulated them, you can post them on my website (www.patriciamarino.com, on the "We the People" tab) so that fruitful conversations can come from them. I am sure that there are fellow Americans who have had similar ideas to mine, or who can add even more to this initial list. Not all of my ideas may be the best approach—some might even be considered naïve, in the end—but as Daniel Burnham said, *Think Big!* And even if we miss the mark sometimes, what will follow will not be a mediocre or miniscule attempt, but rather one that pushes that American Dream ever forward to a re-imagined and re-invigorated country.

Tears to Cheers

The Trail of Tears was just one of hundreds of broken treaties and promises made to the First Peoples encountered by European settlers and explorers, and continued by a federal government intent on a herculean land grab. The removal of Native Americans to often-inhospitable reservations has caused a multitude of problems over centuries, from joblessness to alcoholism. Native Americans have prevailed in many ways, helping their own people to thrive while retaining their native customs and traditions. Beyond the establishment of casinos, Native Americans have managed natural resources as a path towards economic success; and more recently, some tribes manage operations from power plants and vacation travel to agribusiness. As an article on Native American success stories relates, "The three tribes of Oregon's Warm Springs confederation run a series of enterprises that generate $80 million a year in revenue."[66] But they have paid a great cost over the course of our collective history.

The following possibilities offer potential for a nation's healing that might provide a framework of inclusivity. The installation by President Biden of a Native American to run the Department of the Interior and the Bureau of Indian Affairs is an amazing first step.

Native Americans—Specific Concepts

- Rename the Bureau of Indian Affairs (a pejorative term at best)—please! Maybe the "Bureau of Native American Agency," or just the "Native American Agency"? I like the word *agency* because it symbolizes that Native Americans can do for themselves.

- Allow Native Americans who want to, to live in our National Parks, as their ancestors did.

- Expand the number of Native Americans as National Park Rangers who are paid to "steward" the land alongside current park rangers. These jobs also should be open to any American who shares Native Americans' care and concern for Mother Earth.

- Create economic incentives for Native American reservations, beyond casinos and current enterprises, to create new businesses and jobs that work for them.

- Engage Native Americans in the Green Energy Economy and climate-change solutions.

I know that these ideas are painted with a broad brush, with no delineation of how we actually get there. But first we have to imagine "what could be" before we can design the pathway to achieve them.

What *else* could we do? Read on to explore what's possible.

Reparations

Webster's Dictionary defines "reparations" as the act of repairing or the act of making amends, offering expiation, or giving satisfaction for a wrong or injury something done or given as amends or satisfaction.

I have consulted with a good friend—a professor of theology, a minister, and an African American woman—who believes that the more important aspect of reparations is not so much monetary as it is repairing the systems that have prevented the full engagement of African and Native Americans and others of color from participating in the American community. *Repairing* involves activating the full ability of those who have been left out so that they can access the economic, educational, governmental, and other systems, as well as reforming those aspects that still confine certain segments of our society, both literally and figuratively. While I *am* suggesting a monetary reparation in what follows, additional and more substantive reparation needs to come in the form of systems review and revision, and an exploration of the type of revision that makes sense in a constitutional democracy.

Reparations for African Americans

African Americans helped build this country. Plantations in the South that provided extreme wealth to a few landowners were built on the backs of those who worked the cotton and tobacco fields. And while the 1863 Emancipation Proclamation freed those who had been enslaved, African Americans were transformed into a new kind of slavery through Jim Crow laws, which allowed governments essentially to close off both education and economic sources of support. Despite this massive lockout, which included everything from redlining to lynching, African Americans not only survived but also succeeded in many ways—from founding the system of historically Black colleges; to working for civil rights; to founding and continuing successful businesses, from Robert Gordon to Madame C.J. Walker to venture capitalist Reginald Lewis.

Reparations for Native Americans

Native American lands were consistently seized through war, sheer force of guns and soldiers, government decree, and broken treaties too numerous to list—and they are still being broken in the 21st century. The lack of respect for the lands in the Dakotas—for example, when Trump wanted to allow a Canadian company to ship tar-sands oil right across sacred ground without a second thought—is just one example of many today where Native American culture, heritage, rights and respect are still considered "less than."

We as a nation owe African Americans a debt for the 300 years when they were not paid for their labor, and we owe Native Americans a debt for the federal government-sanctioned genocide and land grab. Both these groups have continued to serve this country admirably in war and peace. My dear friend Louie and I argue about this all the time. He states that we would have to start reparations for abuses over the course of centuries in every country, since all of our ancestors have received the short end of the stick at one time or the other; while I argue that providing some sort of reparation (even if small, per person) is significant—not monetarily significant, but as a symbol of our recognition as a nation of the injustices of the past. Such recognition would allow us to move forward. It will be interesting to see how or if this ever comes to fruition.

In the meantime, perhaps more important is enabling African Americans and Native Americans to be fully accepted by all Americans *as* Americans. How reparations might actually be calculated, if there is ever agreement, I leave to the economic wizards. I know that is easier said than done, but that is the necessary trench work. And let's not fall into the trap that the U.S. is facing its greatest deficit ever. If the super-rich and those corporations currently not paying taxes were to pay their fair (not excessive) share, the economic ship would be righted quickly. Reparations and a balanced budget could go hand-in-hand.

Education Re-Thought

Making the History Books Inclusive

For the entire country to be brought together, our history books and curricula need to include the contributions and accurate history of *all* Americans—Native Americans, African Americans, Hispanics, and the many other immigrant contributions that have been made over the years. These contributions should stand with those of their white peers who also contributed much to our values and lives as Americans. While not all Native Americans, African Americans, or immigrants have left an indelible imprint or created significant inventions of thought or materials, many have contributed who have been left out of the history books. Including their contributions in our history would go a long way to reducing the fear of "the other" and putting a mirror up to racism.

I think of myself as a student of history, someone who actually loves this field. And yet I am still astounded at how much I don't know (the histories that never made it into the books) and how much I am learning. Alex's lesson #11 is "Face your fears—know your truth." In researching the economy of the 1950s, I came across the GI Bill, and how much that did for so many to propel them toward better economic growth for themselves and their families. But what else did I learn? That the GI Bill was not much of a benefit to the Black veterans returning from World War II who had fought, and the many who had died, for this country.

> Though the bill helped white Americans prosper and accumulate wealth in the postwar years, it didn't deliver on that promise for veterans of color. In fact, the wide disparity in the bill's implementation ended up helping drive growing gaps in wealth, education and civil rights between white and Black Americans. While the GI Bill's language did not specifically exclude African-American veterans from its benefits, it was structured in a way that ultimately shut doors for the 1.2 million Black veterans who had bravely served their country during World War II, in segregated ranks.[67]

This article, "How the GI Bill's Promise Was Denied to a Million Black WWII Veterans," shows how some of the GI Bill's language was used by realtors who did not want to sell homes to veterans of color in New York, even though they had the same GI-Bill-guaranteed mortgage that other white veterans used to buy homes.

I truly believe that so much of the hate and fear of some Americans towards Black Americans is because much of African American history has been left out of our history books. Facing the truth of our collective history—the good, the bad, and the ugly—will help us to truly know who we are: to celebrate the good and acknowledge the evil, and thereby be free to advance the promise written so long ago by those white men who believed in a better future.

Financial Literacy for All

Financial literacy should be a requisite for all high school students, one that goes beyond the usual one-semester course on budgeting. There should be a four-year requirement for all graduates on economics, investing, the world markets, how the stock market doesn't reflect the real economy, budget planning and forecasting, and much more. Everyone needs to understand their role in making the economy work, and how it can work for all, not just a privileged few. I often wish I had understood much more in this field at a much earlier age.

Civic Education for All

There should be a concerted emphasis on *civic education*, with a focus on:

- The history of democracy
- How a democratic republic works
- The basic foundational structure of checks and balances, and the powers relegated to each branch of government
- The role of the Constitution and the Bill of Rights
- And much more.

While some of this exists in most high school curricula (with greater or less emphasis, depending on the school), civic education has fallen by the wayside. Four-semester courses should be required, perhaps including mock-government legislative sessions, both local and federal.

Rethinking Government Service for Young People

Re-imagine government service in a non-military format. When we think of government service, in the past this has only meant that young men (and now women) should serve in the armed forces. We do, of course, have a volunteer army, which comprises just 0.4% of the U.S. population who "...are overwhelmingly high-quality recruits: they have high school degrees and scored above the fiftieth percentile on the Armed Forces Qualification Test. Most come from middle-class families and have options beyond joining the military. The cohort is young and diverse, and it includes more women than in previous years."[68]

Can we rethink government service for young people? Perhaps it could be a required amount of community service for youth between the ages of 18 and 24 with government or nonprofits in their own communities, which could be fulfilled in over the course of, say, four to six years and would provide community college credit for this service. It also would give young people a chance to work alongside with others who do not necessarily share their interests, ethnic background, or economic level. Perhaps requiring 100-200 hours over six years would go a long way to building understanding of the issues people face, and what is going on in the youths' own communities, whether very local, city, county, region, or state. Hopefully, that experience would remain with these Civic Service youth as they entered college and the workforce. Perhaps a new "GI Bill" (Good Intentions Bill?) could be developed that provides college credit for the service, or funding towards vocational training or college, based on the hours completed, providing a leg-up as the old GI Bill did for veterans.

My caveat is that youth who are learning-challenged (those perhaps with ADD, ADHD, etc.), who have anxiety, mental-health issues, and so on, should be allowed either a different approach (e.g., very local service in their city or town) or complete waivers. Having a child with some of these issues, myself, I know the difficulty they have in going into new or foreign situations, which can exacerbate their disabilities.

Instigate a Massive Communication Strategy

A destructive interweaving of deliberate interferences to democracy has combined to effectively divide this country, divide the politics, silo news information, and turn fact into fiction and fiction into fact. Witness the Russian disinformation campaign in recent years; the Republican party machine to sow distrust of institutions; the gerrymandering of political districts so that representatives don't feel the need to compromise; the perceived disenfranchisement of mostly blue-collar and low-income white workers from the economic engine of America; and non-regulation of social media, combined with the rise of networks purporting to be news outlets, such as Murdoch's Fox News Nation or Opinion or News Max. There needs to be a concerted effort on the part of all our credible communication vehicles to re-establish trust in the profession of journalism (the "fourth estate"), legitimate news organizations, and government. There needs to be a counter-offensive, so to speak—one as sophisticated as the Russians and Fox. The post-Trump era will see the continued rise of media like News Max, a junior version of the old Fox; and if Trump is still around, he will want to continue to be in the limelight and profit from it. A conscious attempt to reach those who aren't cultists (those who haven't yet been co-opted by an extremist group or leader) is imperative for our country to tackle the major problems we face. We need to learn how to talk to each other, and to engage in person as well as through media. Here are some suggestions for ways and programs that that might help to close the fact-divide:

- Fact-based information streams via both local news organizations that might still exist, such as local newspapers, along with more regulated social media outlets.

- An Ambassadors Program—a mixing of urban, suburban, and rural areas with mixed ethnicities, LGBTQ, economic levels, and various regions of the country. I admit that I don't know what this would look like. I just know that when people encounter people in person and have a real conversation with them, the stereotypes and exaggerations often lessen (even if there isn't exactly full acceptance)—whereas in the absence of any interaction, the stereotypes and exaggerations build and expand.

- Support for organizations trying to bring together disparate sides to mend the divisions in this country, such as braverangels.org or similar efforts

- Listening tours by legislators and other government leaders to actually talk with people in a wide range of communities to hear directly their needs and hopes. In short, do a social audit. (This is not rocket science!)

- A concerted effort in town hall meetings across the country to discuss the importance of voting, its history in enabling the voiceless to have voice, and the urgency for Americans to participate at all levels—local, regional, state, and federal.

Political Non-Partisanship

- Place the redistricting of congressional and senatorial districts in the hands of nonpartisan citizen-commissions; take redistricting out of the hands of politicians.

- Overturn the Citizens United Supreme Court decision in 2010, which essentially allows unlimited spending by corporations and special interest groups in elections at all levels. This law reversed almost a century of law that saw the federal government as having a role in preventing political corruption.[69]

- Get the money out of politics. Congress spends more time fundraising than on the issues that need to be addressed because of the exorbitant amount of money needed to fund political races. Consider Senator Elizabeth Warren's Anti-Corruption Plan that she put forth in her run for the presidency; whether you are a Warren fan or not, it makes good sense. A few of these ideas include: Banning foreign corporations from influencing American elections; don't choose Ambassadors based on how much money they donated; ban federal candidates from taking corporate PAC money; and more[70]

- A similar attempt at limiting corruption is the American Anti-Corruption Act—co-authored among others by a former Republican, Trevor Potter, along with many others—that would stop money influencing of politicians, end the "behind closed doors" political contributions, and reform the election system; this was developed in 2011-2012. I haven't done enough research to know the intricacies of this and the perspectives of those behind this legislation, but there are many good ideas out there and they are not just from Democrats or progressives. We need to hear the voices of common sense and non-partisanship.

- Pass the S.2747 Freedom to Vote Act, which would provide federal protection of voting rights in the U.S. and override the state, regional, and local attempts to block voting of the full electorate.

Economic Infusions

- Establish a public-private partnership to catalyze the green economy, along with training programs in both urban and rural communities.

- Ensure that the green economy reaches into low-income urban areas as well as rural areas.

- Establish tax incentives for relocation of businesses to areas of the country that have suffered economically.

- Come up with financial incentives that include broadband access to rebuild infrastructure work around the country.

- Create financial incentives for more efficient public transportation networks and bullet trains connecting major areas of the country.

- Establish a living wage for all Americans as a baseline of support to eradicate or at least ameliorate poverty. This has a direct correlation to lessening crime and catalyzing social and economic improvement. Take a page from the book, Viking Economics by George Lakey

- Establish free public community college and university education as a national policy.

- Revisit and reinvent health care to be cost-free. Also provide new funding for research on diseases and prevention. We can take a cue from how the intense focus on COVID in terms of concentration of time and resources produced vaccines in record time because of both previous research and efforts across the globe.

"The COVID-19 vaccines got a head start from work that's been going on in science for a long time. Scientists have been working on processes for creating all kinds of vaccines for many years. And researchers have been watching and studying corona viruses for decades. They are a very common type of virus. There are hundreds of types of corona virus. And scientists had seen 2 other serious types affect humans just in the past 20 years: SARS and MERS."[71]

There should be a continuation of the global concerted research-effort displayed during COVID, more international cooperation than what I assume has been done in the past.

- Re-establish a mental-health support system that builds on local, community-based organizations. Having mental-health clinics easily accessible and affordable would go a long way to easing the strain that this condition puts not only on families but also on communities, including police forces as a whole

- Provide incentives for medical professionals to serve in low-income communities.

- Establish a Commission on Homelessness to build a national strategy that allows local implementation. This is not about throwing money at a problem, but rather making use of already existing successful community projects as prototypes for a national response.

- Allocate funding to local communities to build housing for the homeless, with social-service components led by and informed by former/current homeless people.

- Create federal incentives for states to build more affordable housing. In California, where I live, housing is a joke. In places like the San Francisco Bay Area, most people struggle just to pay rent or mortgages, let alone food and other necessities.

- Establish a non-partisan Commission on Real Tax Reform with a brain trust across political lines to ensure that the tax system is fair to all and does not place undue burdens on the poor and middle class (which has been the standard for the past 50 years).

New Ways to Think about Policing

The suggestions that follow come from my observations, from incidents occurring over the past thirty years, and from information from a trusted veteran police officer with 30+ years' experience in a major metropolitan area.

First, there are good cops everywhere, so they need to be supported.

Second, it is regretful that the term "defund the police" was used, because the right wing jumped on that immediately to again stoke the fear we all have of being on the wrong end of a gun or defenseless in the face of criminals. What was meant by this term was to rethink policing, and to use funds to address nonviolent crimes in a more humane, thoughtful, and successful way, rather than shooting to kill when not necessary. Some recommendations include:

- Pass gun legislation that takes automatic weapons off the streets (for a start; eventually include hand guns). And no, I am not talking here about taking guns from those who hunt animals, just from the ones hunting human beings. There is a place for those duck, deer, and other legal animal hunters. But using an AK 47 or other military weapons to hunt animals, let alone people, is not considered "sporting" by any stretch of the imagination.

- Improve the hiring process, and make it as intensive and subject to scrutiny as it once was. The recruiting process needs to demand high-quality personnel from the beginning, weeding out potential ill-informed thinking and behavior. (Translation: racist, bigoted thinking and violent behavior.)

- Retrain our police forces—based on a de-escalation model used in some areas of our own country and in other parts of the world—as the major approach, with a back-up force that does carry weapons. There was a time when cops fired their weapons not to kill but to bring down a potential perpetrator, such as shooting in the knee or leg. But there have been too many examples of excessive use of force, of late. When did it become open season to shoot to kill *all* the time? If firing one bullet will do the job, is dumping multiple rounds of bullets into someone really necessary?

- Re-imagine policing. Perhaps look at the firefighters' work structure—72 hours on call, 48 hours off. I understand that this may not work because of the nature of police work, but what about three 10-hour shifts on and two shifts off? There should be a daily 1-hour debriefing session before police officers check out. And mental health should be high on any police department's self-regulating radar because of the incredibly stressful nature of this work.

- Can we reform the criminal justice system once and for all? Can we again engage a brain trust from all levels—federal and local—to rethink the structure?

- Do we really need private prison operations?

- While some cities (such as Oakland, CA) still need more police officers, we need to engage police who are part of the community, who know their neighborhoods in order to build that trust. There are some models around the country that could be replicated. Think about the following:

  « Nationwide, an estimated 80% of 911 calls are made for nonviolent, non-property offenses, says Frankie Wunschel, a research associate at the Vera Institute. The *New York Times* found that the share of time officers spend handling violent crime this year in New Orleans, Sacramento, CA, and Montgomery County, MD was only 4%.[72]

« Eugene, Oregon with its CAHOOTS model (Crisis Assistance Helping Out On the Streets), reviewed by cities such as Denver, New York City, Portland, and Oakland, CA can inform how we support police work while also addressing nonviolent crime.

- Establish a Prison-to-Work Employment training program for non-violent offenders to reduce recidivism. This requires a public-private partnership, to ensure that the stigma of being an ex-convict is addressed. And support employers that hire.

- Engage nonprofit, community-based organizations that employ models like CAHOOTS to respond to police calls which are really more mental-health situations. This frees the police for serious, violent situations.

Some Afterthoughts

I know that it's easy to offer suggestions, that coming up with ideas is easier than making them real; and maybe some of these recommendations might even be seen as simplistic. Rest assured that I do acknowledge the hard work involved in making even minor changes within complicated systems that have been crafted over decades. The Affordable Care Act, for one, didn't spring up overnight; I am sure that it took numerous innovative minds and technical experts to craft this legislation over years. In the course of its implementation, there have been hiccups, and it still needs adjusting; but it appears that the American people like it. Again, the above are simply springboard suggestions for the purpose of eliciting *your* thoughts.

These thoughts and suggestions were born from my experiences as a teacher and as someone who has observed the day-in/day-out work of nonprofits (too numerous to count) in the San Francisco Bay Area, primarily the East Bay, as they tackle the tough job of addressing education, homelessness, mental health, teens in trouble, the lack of arts and arts education, gang violence, and so much more. My observations come from a lifetime of work in the philanthropy field, as well. As much as I have seen the not-so-good in humanity, every day I also see the "trench work," as I call it, of so many organizations that hold out a helping hand and provide quality, effective programs that are literally saving lives every day—quietly, without fanfare, just "doing their jobs."

For example, because I have had professional dealings with the Boys & Girls Club, I was able to hear the story about a Hispanic mother whose three very young sons were going to a local chapter. At the same time, she had to go to kidney dialysis three times weekly. During COVID, her husband had a stroke, and she had to go to work to support the family despite her doctors saying she should not. She talked about how fantastic it was that her three children could be in an after-school program that provided them with support, fun, and great programs. It helped her not to have to worry about their well-being.

As it turned out, she passed away not long after she had talked about the program. The children now live with their grandfather while the husband is still dealing with the impact of his stroke. They still attend the Club program, and the Club staff care for those children as if they are their own—which, in the communal sense, they are. We are all our brothers' keepers. In communities across this country, such acts of support, kindness, and caring get played out daily. These acts help to ensure that this country, and the children who will become the adults of this country, are able to continue the better part of the heritage we all share.

It is easy to fall into the trap of despair and hopelessness, the belief that there is nothing we can do. When *I* find myself worrying that the problems in this country are overwhelming, I think about the resilience of the people in my family—my Dad, my Mom, my extended family (Vito, Grace, Frances, Lena, Uncles Pete, Jaspar, Larry, Nick, Joe, cousin Honey, Aunt Mary, and my other Aunt Mary—remember, this is an *Italian* family: why choose another name when the same one will do?—and so many cousins). I remember their perseverance, their ability to find humor in daily life, their joy in the simple things that made life worth living; their going for their version of the American Dream. Alex was definitely a problem solver and did not brook bullshit. He called it as he saw it, and tried to always see the larger issue, what was the right thing to do, even if it meant bucking the powers that be. While I have been known to use some of his expletives when the moment calls for it, that part of my Dad doesn't usually come out in me. But his strength, his grit, his ability to go straight to the heart of the matter, his not letting others' view of Italians (let alone Sicilians) stand in his way—all this seeped into my bones over the years.

These traits stood me in good stead when I worked with gang kids in Chicago; when I taught students from around the City and the globe in San Francisco's south-of-Market neighborhood; and when I worked in corporate America (which was a different type of terrain), where keeping my own name caused a few furrows in brows, and where I told the truth in the face of losing my job and more.

I know that Alex has been right there with me all along, helping me to give as good as I get. I am just like everyone else who comes from immigrants, whether recently or in the very distant past—those immigrants, those slaves, those Native Americans, each of them seeking to name their own path, their life journey, in a country with a Dream that allows for transformation.

It's still a good Dream. We just have to make that transformation available to everyone.

Where Are We in Our Country? A Gut Check

While the ideas I am suggesting in this chapter are a lot to chew on, they do provide us with food for thought, and more. We need a gut check on where we are as a country. There is a part of our history that needs addressing now—the slavery and genocide. Facing the disenfranchisement of our past doesn't mean that we can't honor the rest of our history, the valuable traditions we have, and the good in our country and its citizens. Knowing the whole truth informs our path in the present and the future. But we have to have the courage to acknowledge the past, the wrongs done, so that we can embrace the future fully. **Lesson #11 = Face Your Fears and Your Truth.**

There are as many ways to tackle the existential threats to America today as there are creative souls with talent, strength, and wisdom to bring to bear on these threats. We face enormous challenges right now. If we are to wake up and change the American Dream into a new American reality—one that sets the course for the *next* millennium—then we need all hands on deck, not just the select few.

CHAPTER 10

Beloved Community

A Nostalgia for Community

Looking back at the decisions I made, I can see that many of them were made because of my Dad's tenacity and willingness to figure out next steps, to take a chance on something. While he did this in the context of living in the same neighborhood and City all his life, his attitude was always about figuring out how to right the ship, how to fix things—not to make the mistake of not trying something different, even though some of his "tries" did not work out.

For those who are still to add their piece to the American mosaic, for whom the American Dream has been given only begrudgingly but not robustly—the forgiveness, compassion, and love that my Dad had in his life and which he gave to others needs to be magnified now more than ever. It's clear that fighting for what is right and just must walk alongside love, not hate; understanding, not resentment; healing, not revenge.

While talking to my brother the other day, I heard in his voice a longing, a nostalgia for a time and place so long ago for our family and community in Chicago. Chicago was (and I believe still is) a place of neighborhoods, each with its own character—its own *characters*—food, and languages. Our neighborhood long ago was anchored by an Irish bar (a pub, really) to which, on many Fridays, much of the neighborhood gathered—the ethnic diversity at the time, and Jews, Protestants, and Catholics. The Catholics, of course, ate fish on Friday, while the rest of the crew could eat meat (which we in the Catholic category deemed wholly unfair). The bar was tended by a sometimes loveable, often gruff old curmudgeon named Mike D.—who, if he didn't know you, didn't like the way you looked, or didn't like the look you gave him, wouldn't serve you and would summarily throw you

Dad and Mom, July 1960

out. If, however, you were in his good graces, he could be incredibly kind. It was indeed a local bar. Fridays, families came to the bar and, amidst the food and drink and Irish music and songs, the neighborhood came together. The smoke hung over the rooms, the smells of Mrs. D.'s cooking permeated the walls, and kids ran everywhere while adults shared their stories of the week, their heartaches, and laughter. St. Paddy's Day was a big deal. This was my Dad and Mom's world.

I think it was a solace place, a refuge from the realities of rent (they never owned their own home while I was growing up), broken promises and dreams; a place where they could have a fun time with friends. The circle of friends they had there was amazing—probably at least 20 couples whom they were close to, and all centered around our parish. Our parish was probably the safest place to grow up in the City, since about a dozen policemen lived there, along with assorted "others" who lived a quiet life, post-mob work. I remember my parents' lively parties in our basement, with the music playing, an "open bar," dancing through the night, and lots of laughter.

That love of gathering, of parties, linked back to both my grandmother and grandfather on Cambridge Avenue, with neighbors, relatives, and local merchants and pols stopping by. This continued with my Grandmother's birthday (which was around New Year's Eve), my

Dad's birthday (on December 16th) and my mother's (on December 27th). All the local merchants came, and kids were allowed to stay up until Otto the neighborhood butcher put on his roller skates and skated around the basement playing his accordion (Otto loved the schnapps!). Harold Losby, our local drug store owner and pharmacist, was there, and many others, as well.

I think Alexander Francis felt at home here. My Mom and Dad's world was a tight-knit community around our Catholic Church and school. But it also included Losby's Drugstore, run by Harold Losby and his wife; Schroeder's Bakery; and Mr. Sheerin's Soda Fountain. The neighborhood was knitted with local businesses, public and Catholic schools, churches, and parks into a community life that was both vibrant and embracing—sometime suffocating, because you were known in the neighborhood, but nonetheless a great way to grow up.

Alexander Francis (as I wrote, when this journey of a book first started) taught me many things, from street smarts to speaking truth to power. But more than anything, he taught me about love and kindness—very powerful ammunition to have in the struggle of life. While he did not use a lot of fancy words (he probably more often was comfortable with "other" words), he was a very bright man with a big heart. His help ranged from small gestures like lending a friend money—there was no "loan" agreement, with interest rates identified and forms to fill out with some bank—to not thinking twice about hopping a plane from Chicago to California to solve a friend's family situation, a daughter in trouble. The young woman's father was distraught and didn't know what to do. I guess Mr. F. felt that my Dad's long-dormant Chicago-detective experience would go a long way to expediting his wish to bring his daughter home.

I never knew the circumstances or the reasons for the daughter's move there. But whatever afflicted her soul and spirit—perhaps family issues, who knows?—she gradually devolved into hard-core drug use. Alex had seen much of what drugs like heroin could do to a human being in the course of his work, so he knew first-hand the consequences that would ensue if the drug use was not stopped.

Since my Dad rarely traveled beyond Michigan, Wisconsin, and Indiana (Louisiana was a big trip), a trip to California was highly unusual. But Alex didn't hesitate. He jumped on the plane and found his friend's daughter at the apartment address in California he had been given. I am sure he used his powerful persuasive abilities, plus who knows what financial incentives the father had offered, to convince her to return home. Regardless of her long-term outcome—hopefully, a more positive future—Alexander took time out of his own life to help a friend who was asking a huge favor.

Despite my Dad's tough exterior, I understood his heart, even when he was down. I always thought how difficult it must have been to have once been a successful detective and part of a thriving family business, and then subsequently be unable to continue in that business because of illness; how difficult it must have been to have tried afterwards, in multiple ways and multiple times, to reboot that American Dream by starting a real estate business, or by investing in gas wells. His life ended working as a salaried employee, with impoverished souls trying to scrape by to make ends meet. In that situation, I believe he saw no color or status, but rather human beings who needed help with a system that wasn't always fair.

There is a nostalgia for that era of the 1950s and 1960s, post-World War II, when the middle class thrived and the economy boomed; when there was a post-war collective psyche rejoicing in a system of normalcy. For many in that era, it was an idyllic world, one that was both safe and prosperous. As kids, we could walk to school, use public transportation to see friends or explore the City, and visit parks on the outskirts of the City (the Forest Preserves); as teens, we could search for jobs. This is not to be naïve: there were places where you just did not go, and there was crime, evil, and corruption percolating in areas of the City. My Dad knew that all too well from his time on the force. In many neighborhoods during that era, however, there was safety and a feeling of community.

And Some Not-So-Nostalgic Aspects

For some populations, however, there were whole neighborhoods in the City as well as other communities around the country where finding a decent job was not the norm—where it was a matter of fearing for your life, of seeing crosses burning on your lawn, of limitations to access to certain areas of hotels, restaurants, and buses; of signs announcing, "no Blacks need apply" and "colored water fountain"—all this, too, was life *de rigueur*. These were loud and clear signs that Blacks, Hispanics, Native Americans, and some other immigrants were not welcome. It was more blatant in the Southern states, but it also existed (though more subtly—sometimes) in the North and West.

Sinatra certainly encountered this disequilibrium in American society in the course of his entertainment travels. Racism was as specific in New York City as it was in Atlanta, and as virulent on the West Coast as it was on the East Coast. The reality for those American citizens who have stood by America while being locked out of its benefits has long been unaddressed. This book's focus on African Americans and Native Americans does not mean that immigrants who came to these shores of their own free will or as indentured servants long ago did not struggle, and that the newly arrived don't struggle as well. It doesn't mean that others—for example, in the rust belts of America who have lost jobs, or in rural areas that have seen businesses leave and towns boarded up—didn't have their own struggles. Those realities need to be addressed in this American Dream re-imagining, as well. The key to this re-imagining is to include everyone—*all* Americans.

That push to include all Americans was never so dramatically on display as during the awful, strange, and confining year 2020, with protests across the country. The Black Lives Matter protests against police brutality—the use of excessive force, and the killing of so many Black and brown people in just that one year—catalyzed a cross-section of America to rise up and say: "Enough is enough!" There was a lot of "good trouble," as U.S. Congressman and long-time civil rights advocate John Lewis would say—an anger and frustration about justice long denied; a fear of the "noise" made, of the uncertainty caused by the disease and devolution of justice on many levels: political, economic, legal, and social. Lewis' insistence on making enough "good trouble" to change society and move it forward has been and probably will continue to be emphasized as we move ourselves closer to a new American Dream.

Yet while a great deal of our history is rightly focused on the *wrongs* done, the other element exemplified by John Lewis—which we might be in danger of forgetting about—was his insistence on *love and forgiveness*, which he practiced throughout his life. He was the chairman of the Student Nonviolent Coordinating Committee when, in 1965, he protested against police violence along with others. What he met on the Edmund Pettus Bridge that day was violence itself: police battered his head and inflicted great pain on his body. The son of sharecroppers, Lewis could have easily become bitter and angry. Instead, he became the *embodiment* of the American Dream, taking each hand dealt him, each blow (both physically and mentally), and returning that with yes, action, but also with love. He rose to become one of the most positive and productive members of the U.S. Congress.

Prejudice has played out over the course of our history among those who—although they knew that what they were doing was wrong, morally and legally—had the upper hand economically and politically, and thus gave birth to the long reach of Jim Crow laws. There were also many mostly good people, I am sure, with their foibles and prejudices, who were focused on their day-to-day lives. Those prejudices played out against other immigrant groups they didn't understand, as well as African Americans and Native Americans—prejudices that grew out of the ignorance of their respective histories and contributions; out of media stereotypes, played out in print and films of the day; out of racist theories based in myth (aka the "pure race" of Hitler and his Nazis); and out of fear. Such people were neither the architects of Jim Crow nor would many have actually participated in violence; but their prejudices were there.

Understanding them doesn't excuse them; but their prejudice was based in fear of the "unknown," in fear of "they don't look like us," in fear of the redlining myth—and just sheer ignorance. The hurt caused by their actions was, and is, a pain that doesn't go away. There is a deep, centuries-old need for accountability and a cry for justice; there is anger, bitterness, and hatred of the white systemic racism that has blocked Blacks and Native Americans from economic and social success. The rumblings of this long-dormant volcano of unaddressed resentment, past violence, enslavement, and economic bondage has exploded in the American national psyche. And rightfully so, with a whole swath of the American community saying, "NO MORE, NEVER AGAIN!"

John Lewis' call for forgiveness does not in any way let white supremacy off the hook. Far from it—such forgiveness calls for facing the truth and rectifying the injustice. The systemic racism that permeates so many American institutions—from banking to housing to education to social media—necessitates enormous, intentional steps in order to course-correct. Yet the sheer massiveness of the task should not deter us as a country. The first steps were taken with the Civil Rights Act in 1965, and there have been starts and stops along the way. We as a nation are in a great period of transformation, and we need courage to right the wrongs of that post-Civil War era, which have continued in many ways into own our time.

Each action in service of this course-correction is a step in the right direction. Reparations, for example, constitute one tangible way of acknowledging the genocide and horrific acts of violence that have spanned 400 years. Facing both our fears and the truth should lead to a more inclusive, welcoming community, one that emphasizes justice married with forgiveness—a kind of two-headed Janus, looking back to remember and rectify, but also looking forward to realize and re-imagine.

Forgiveness is a very hard, almost impossible road to take. I remember the businessman who told me I would never succeed in business, that I should just "go home and have kids." Or how, when I was looking to change my work position, I applied to a local foundation and was told by the executive director, "I would hire you in a minute, but you are the wrong color" (meaning white). I was furious about both these responses, and certainly didn't want to forgive either person. But these were infinitesimal insults, compared to the outright and ever-present prejudice that those who are not white have faced for their entire lives. Yet if we don't include forgiveness in our reparations-and-revisioning effort, we run the risk of exacerbating the problem. Then, those who can't forgive become "the unforgiven." Focusing only on hate, the negative, the hurt attracts only hate, negativity, and hurt.

At the same time, there has to be active resistance to evil, a righting of wrongs, in whatever form that takes. Conviction of crimes against humanity, as well as reparations, must be realized. Forgiveness is not a simple matter. I, for one, am still struggling with balancing the need for justice long denied and forgiving those who have perpetrated evil that no human should ever have to endure. Recently, I had a discussion with a friend about forgiveness for atrocities. If her family had been killed in World War II, would she have been able to forgive the Nazis who did it? For my part, if one of *my* family had been sent to a gas chamber, I don't know that I could find that forgiveness in my heart. Or if my son had been Ahmaud Arbery, a totally innocent Black man out for a jog one day who was killed by three white men, would I be able to find forgiveness? What was in the cultural and emotional backgrounds of these three men? What racist propaganda had they been fed, embedded in their culture, that created such hate and fear? We all know that if a white man had been jogging, nothing would have happened. So even as I write about forgiveness in the broad sense, I am still struggling with the balance, personally, whether I could forgive someone who shot my brother or sister for no reason other than the color of their skin.

It's important to keep in mind that forgiveness does not excuse the sin, or the sinner; rather, what it does do is release those who were wronged from continuing to carry the bondage of hurt and pain. As Shakespeare wrote: *"The quality of mercy is not strained; it droppeth as the gentle rain from heaven upon the place beneath. It is twice blest; it blesseth him that gives and him that takes."* Like mercy, forgiveness has a dual blessing: it blesses the forgiver as well as the forgiven. Maintaining hatred and bitterness only gives power to the abuser; it enables that person to still have some sway over you, some way of still hurting you, to still control what happens in your life emotionally or mentally. "We've got to be as clear-headed about human beings as possible, because we are still each other's only hope," James Baldwin told Margaret Mead in their historic conversation about forgiveness.[73] Love moves us forward; hate does not. "I have decided to stick to love; hate is too great a burden to bear," said Martin Luther King.[74]

John Lewis knew profoundly that the human race cannot move forward in hate and divisiveness; that only when we can muster forgiveness will true healing begin. "Our actions entrench the power of the light on this planet. Every positive thought we pass between us makes room for more light. And if we do more than think, then our actions clear the path for even more light. That is why forgiveness and compassion must become more important principles in public life."[75]

Forgiveness and compassion, however, have to be part of *every* aspect of our lives, not just public life. That's why I brought up "capitalism with a conscience." Proponents of any good respectable economic model that wants to be around for the long term understand that *all* need to share in the rewards of the economy, not just a few—because the "all-sharing" model builds the economy, moves it forward. Just as the stock market doesn't reflect the real economy, so—in the long view of history—making a few people ultra-rich will not sustain the economic model. Economically, socially, and intellectually, compassion and forgiveness need to be embedded in the way we live, privately and publicly. Lewis went on to say:

> Anchor the eternity of love in your own soul and embed this planet with goodness. Lean toward the whispers of your own heart, discover the universal truth, and follow its dictates. Release the need to hate, to harbor division, and the enticement of revenge. Release all bitterness. Hold only love, only peace in your heart, knowing that the battle of good to overcome evil is already won. Choose confrontation wisely, but when it is your time don't be afraid to stand up, speak up, and speak out against injustice. And if you follow your truth down the road to peace and the affirmation of love, if you shine like a beacon for all to see, then the poetry of all the great dreamers and philosophers is yours to manifest in a nation, a world community, and a Beloved Community that is finally at peace with itself.[75]

My Family's Own Beloved Community

Throughout this book, I have been painting a portrait of my father—not only the lessons I learned from him, but also his actual personality and values—that, to me, is just the way it was. Alex was strong, compassionate, vital, truthful, and much more, and his relationship to those in power was uncowed. Nevertheless, I can imagine my brother reading this book and shaking his head in puzzlement, then setting me straight: "What planet are you from??? Dad was a much more aggressive, vitriolic, Type A personality than you have portrayed him."

Alex *was* all of that—a hyperbole in spades. He loved his curse words, was energy personified, moved quickly, loved to dance, and held strong views (including prejudices)—he was all of that. I remember a time in my twenties when my Dad got furiously angry with me after he had gone to the trouble of securing me a teaching position at a local neighborhood high school within walking distance of our two-flat, just in time for me to start as I returned home in the summer of 1969 from a visit to my then-boyfriend (later, husband) in California. Having already worked as a bank teller in California for about four months, I told Alex that I wasn't taking the teaching job; that I was going back to California. My brother's view was borne out, writ large: anger swelled up in my Dad to the point where he could hardly spit out the words; and once he was able, he cursed a blue streak as only he could do. In fact, he became so visibly agitated that my brother had to physically force him to sit down.

So yes, Alex was not prone to encourage his daughter to choose her own career. He was Old School in many ways, including his views of a woman's place in society and what a woman's role should be: you didn't move out of your parents' house unless and until you married. But even then, I understood that his anger erupted not only because he had gotten me the teaching job by asking a favor of an old friend who worked at the school, but also that (in his view) I was just being stupid about my future. I also knew that it was hard for him to articulate his feelings—that he was no more capable of telling me, "I'm worried for you because I love you" than he was of softening into tears. So while, on the surface, his reaction made *me* angry, I also realized that the baseline for all his angst was love. He wanted a better future for me, an easier path than the one he'd had to take.

Anger was one area where my brother would not have been off-base to question my largely positive portrait of my Dad. When Alex got angry like that, we nicknamed him "Alex the Terrible." Such volatility was displayed frequently in Dad's final, post-retirement, job—assisting a friend's young son who was managing a restaurant in downtown Chicago. When Alex had finally retired at the age of 67, within the first four months of retirement he was already getting into my mother's hair (and her kitchen). She called an old family friend to ask if there was a part-time job that would occupy Alex for at least a part of the week; the friend's son had a restaurant, and thus the restaurant gig.

On the day my Dad died from a massive heart attack in June 1975, they found him at the bottom of the stairs in the restaurant, holding something in his hand and with a large welt on his forehead. Everyone assumed that the welt came from his falling down the stairs. However, the story we heard later was that he was so angry about something the young restaurateur had done that he felt obliged to give his take on what *should* be done—all the while gesticulating with a ladle in his hand—and that he had actually hit himself in the head very hard, on purpose, as if to make the point that the son was being a "hard head" (or, as the Italians say, *testa dura*, when someone isn't listening to advice).

Yet Alex was really Alex the *Compassionate*, as well—a compassion he showed his own family, his friends, distant relatives, perfect strangers, and his neighborhood throughout his entire life. My sister recently told me a story about how Alex, in one of his many jobs following his Chicago detective life as a bailiff for the local court system, would work with the court on behalf of children convicted of misdemeanors to have their records expunged. He was fiercely protective of children and did not want to see youthful mistakes affecting their adulthood. And because of Dad's background as an electrician and his carpentry skills, he would often help friends or relatives with home projects that they couldn't figure out—usually at no cost to them, since he figured that it was just his time he was spending. (My mother would often complain that *our* home should be on his "to do list.") Yes, he *was* embittered about not having achieved the kind of American Dream he had envisioned in his twenties and thirties, about the kind of material success he had tasted for a brief while and then lost. But he never wavered in the love of his family, or his willingness to try to right the ship—even to the very end, when he had a part-time job managing a friend's son's restaurant to make ends meet.

By all counts, Alex and our family had a decent life. We got to grow up in a stable neighborhood, with friends and family that we loved, and a real sense of community. It was Alex's *love* that was my greatest lesson in life, one that I have taken with me through the journey of years, no matter the roads that twisted and turned.

After I passed on that cushy teaching job back in the early 1970s and chose to stay in California for about six months, Al and I were married and Al decided to study law at Northwestern; so back to Chicago it was. I took up the title of "breadwinner," working in a variety of teaching positions at both public and private high schools during our short years of residence in the City, while also studying for my Master's degree at the University of Illinois. I received a terminal Master's, since I had to re-take one test, which I put off on the basis of just not having enough time to study. The teaching jobs weren't easy ones—in one instance, working with gang kids, traveling by bus further west to another high school. It would have been far easier to have taken that teaching job my Dad had arranged close to home; it would have been an easier group of students to work with, and I could have walked to work! When Al finished several years at Northwestern and we moved from Chicago back to his hometown in California, I searched for teaching positions, and took a job in a demonstration program under the San Francisco Community College District. At the same time, I volunteered part-time for a State Senator and his staff, who taught me lots of new skills, supported me, and recommended me to a public affairs training program, the Coro Foundation. This ultimately led to a 30-plus-year career in philanthropy, learning about the world of nonprofits (the "Independent Sector") and foundations. Because of the Senator's and his staff's careful tutelage of me, I was able to transition to another world where I could still help support education and young people, using my background as a teacher and pulling many strands of my interests and work together into one career.

Looking back at those decisions I made, I can see that many of them were made because of my Dad's tenacity and willingness to figure out next steps, to take a chance on something. While he did this in the context of living in the same neighborhood and City all his life, his attitude was always about figuring out how to right the ship, how to fix things—not to make the mistake of not trying something different, even though some of his "tries" did not work out.

I probably gave him some of his heart attacks by pushing the envelope and doing some of my "tries" in a larger context, looking beyond Chicago. Going to Rome was one of those "test cases." I was a commuter student for my first two years of college; my parents were able to pay for some tuition (I had a scholarship, also) but not for board. The John Felice Rome Center, Loyola University, Chicago, was a relatively new program, and one that I was eager to try. I wanted to taste a bit of being "on campus"—but that campus was 8,000 miles away. I can still remember my Dad and Mom walking me out to the chartered KLM flight and asking me, as I was set to walk up the stairs to the plane, "You are really not going, are you? Nine months?" I saw the disbelief in my Dad's eyes, and, I am sure, anxiety about what could happen to his daughter. But what I would want to say to him now was that his toughness, *his* courage gave *me* the courage to take that step to get on that flight to Rome. That first step out of my comfort zone led to many other such first steps, each one taken with the strength and skills I had learned from him.

We did indeed have a Beloved Community, long ago. I know Alex did not understand the world that began to change in the 1960s or care for it much. He thought the protesters at the Democratic convention should be thrown in jail, that Vietnam War protestors were just a bunch of hippies who didn't have much to keep them busy, and on and on. I do think part of this was again fear of the unknown, of "what's happening to how things used to be"—the uncertainty, and the faces of those who look different. I say this not to excuse him, but to better understand who he was: the son of immigrants who came looking for a better life. Alex and his family—my Uncle Pete, Uncle Larry, Uncle Nick, Aunt Lena, Aunt Frances, Uncle Jasper, Uncle Vito and Aunt Grace, Aunt Mary, Uncle Joe—all contributed (in their own small, day-to-day way) to the life that we know as American. Their names won't be recorded anywhere but in a cemetery and this book, for their contributions were like those of so many who came before them and will come again. They raised children, paid taxes, and in so many ways helped to add their piece of the mosaic that makes up the fabric of this country. They formed community and passed it on to the next generation. They gave love to their family and that community.

For those who are still to add their piece to the American mosaic, for whom the American Dream has been given only begrudgingly but not robustly—the forgiveness, compassion, and love that my Dad had in his life and which he gave to others needs to be magnified now more than ever. In the midst of the cowardice of some elected officials, of the broken pieces of an American Dream stunted in its growth, of white supremacists' hatred, of media moguls who twist the truth to make bigger profits, it's clear that fighting for what is right and just must walk alongside love, not hate; understanding, not resentment; healing, not revenge.

Alex valued fairness . . . smarts . . . speaking truth to power . . . community . . . doing right, in the real sense . . . and yes, love, in his own limited way. His gifts helped me on my journey from that small neighborhood in Chicago into the larger world, which is certainly complex and fraught with division and challenges. But if everyone is to have a chance at that Beloved Community—the *real* American Dream—then in a fractured world we all need to be a juggernaut for justice, love, and peace. We need to be collective "artists" adding our particular, unique pieces to the American mosaic as a whole, "...because we are still each other's only hope."

CHAPTER 11

Lessons from America

Reflections on Adding Your Pieces to the American Mosaic

Truth and facts are a good place to start. So here are some questions to get your reflections and suggestions going.

Thank you, Readers, for taking this journey with me through my own family, my past, to better understand these times we are in and how my family's history relates to the bigger picture of the American Dream. But my story is just one of hundreds of thousands over the centuries.

Rather than only revisiting *my* neighborhood, *my* place in time, I think it is important to hear *your* stories, *your* reflections, *your* suggestions—for a stronger, more vibrant economy; for an engaged, supported, and contributing middle and working class; for the potential to solve some of our most urgent problems; for how we engage as global citizens. I learned a lot from my Dad, my Mother, and the rest of my family. Perhaps you have lessons learned from your *own* family that you might want to share—lessons that would fire our imagination and creativity, that would provide insights into how we can go about making this a fairer, more just American community.

I am interested, as well, in your feelings about how we could build a more Beloved Community in your *own* neighborhood, among your *own* friends and family. It seems to me that over time we have become too separated, too much in our own worlds. Many of the suggestions I made in Chapter 9 involved actions that the government could take. Equally important, however, is how we as individuals can take actions in our own communities to improve the lives for all who live there—not just in formal ways, but also in everyday informal ways. How do we bring everyone into the conversation, even those who are on the extremes?

Truth and facts are a good place to start. So here are some questions to get your reflections and suggestions going.

Reflections on Your Family

- Who were or are they?
- Where did they emigrate from, and when?
- Why did they come?
- What were their struggles, or are their struggles now?
- How did they cope with the foreignness of our culture compared to the one they left behind?
- What were, or are, their joys?
- What, in their minds, was the "American Dream"?
- How did your family background or origin display itself in terms of the American Dream?
- What has been your "inheritance" from your family about the American Dream?
  - « What parts would you choose to keep?
  - « What part of this does *not* reflect you, or the person you want to become, or the country in which you want to live?

Reflections on Re-Thinking the American Dream

"You have noticed that everything an Indian does is in a circle, and that is because the Power of the World always works in circles, and everything tries to be round. In the old days when we were a strong and happy people, all our power came to us from the sacred hoop of the nation, and so long as the hoop was unbroken, the people flourished... But the Wasichus ["greedy ones"—i.e., white people] have put us in these square boxes. Our power is gone and we are dying, for the power is not in us

any more... Well, it is as it is. We are prisoners of war while we are waiting here. But there is another world."

—Black Elk, in *Black Elk Speaks*[76]

The great experiment that is America is the willingness to open doors to humanity in all its shapes and sizes, colors and genders, and the trust that from many comes one: *E Pluribus Unum* (as is inscribed on most denominations of U.S. currency). It's a remarkable theory, considering that so much of human history has been about fighting to keep people out, to have one group rule over the rest, to concentrate power and money in the hands of a few. The American Dream is truly mind-bending, when you really think about it. But reality hasn't always matched the myth.

- Given your family's history, struggles, achievements, and aspirations, what might a re-envisioned, re-thought American Dream might look like?
- Who is missing from the potential of the Dream?
- What would a re-imagined Dream look like to you?

Reflections on the Vision of a New American Dream

Think about what you have inherited from your family's venture in this country. Add that to your own experiences, whether you are the immigrant, the first generation, the second generation, or continuing generations, the descendant of slaves, or of Native Americans. What have been your experiences, your observations of how things work in this country? What would you like to see happen—what are your aspirations for a New American Dream?

- What is your vision for the American Dream?
- In practical terms, what are some real-world applications for your vision—real-world solutions that you would like to see applied?
  - « In your own personal life?
  - « In public life through government policies?
  - « In the economy?

« In education?

« Where else?

While we are envisioning a new construct for the American Dream, perhaps we can also think about what that means in terms of our collective responsibility to our neighbors, our community, and the Constitution. What has been so disturbing to me is when people in the U.S. talk about their individual rights without understanding that we are part of a *larger* community—a federation of states, a republic. While the Constitution does protect a great deal of individual rights— freedom of religion, speech, and more—it does not protect individual rights at all costs, to the exclusion of the next person.

So when you are thinking about your vision of the American Dream, also think about what are our *collective responsibilities to each other*—to the larger community—in order to ensure that the promise of the Declaration of Independence and the Constitution comes to realize a nation in harmony with itself through compassion, empathy, and the application of rights to all, not just selectively.

This is the brainstorming section for you to think broadly and, at the same time, locally.

- What could you do on a very personal level to help move the American Dream closer to a reality for everyone?

- How, in your day-to-day life, can you open the door for someone else—maybe someone who doesn't have your background, experience, or benefits from the kind of network you have that supports your daily life in terms of both your work and family life?

- What are the kinds of conversations you can begin to have with co-workers, friends, family, neighbors about binding the wounds of community disintegration?

- What are the lessons you learned in your family that, by your sharing them, can provide a helping hand to those who are struggling, those who have not been able to fully participate in this American Dream?

- Could we begin to build a storyboard across this country of inclusion rather than exclusion? Of telling the truth, of getting facts right, of building bridges for assimilation, not barricades?

- Could we develop an American Dream website where your ideas can potentially have a wider audience, with postings of real results, from conversations to communal action? In the section of my website that I am dedicating towards this end, your contributions will help to make all this real. (See the "We the People" page on my website, *www.patriciamarino.com*)

Think about all this as you help this country begin to complete that American Dream, that experiment now 245 years in the making.

Epilogue

Lessons Learned in the Alexander Francis School of Life and Their Translation to a Re-Imagined American Dream

Seeking the fulfillment of the American Dream for everyone in this country takes understanding our past, knowing where we come from, understanding that at one time or another our ancestors were considered "the other."

> O, yes,
> I say it plain,
> America never was America to me,
> And yet I swear this oath—
> America will be!
> Out of the rack and ruin of our gang-
> ster death,
> The rape and rot of graft, and
> stealth, and lies,
> We, the people, must redeem
> The land, the mines, the plants, the rivers.
> The mountains and the endless plain—
> All, all the stretch of these great
> green states—
> And make America again!
>
> —Langston Hughes,
> "Let America Be America Again"

As I draw together my reflections on the lessons I learned in the Alexander Francis school of life, I find keys as to how we might approach rebuilding the American Dream for all, not just a privileged few.

It is imperative that we take a diligent review of those laws that hold people back, that we look for the "right" in what is codified, not just the legal (**Lesson #1: Laws Don't Always Equal Right**). Many of us are taught in school or by our families early on to be accountable for our actions; but often this is disregarded; or accountability is only for a portion of the population, not applied across the board.

We have to call out the hypocrisy in the lack of accountability today for those in power who hide behind technicalities and do not take the moral or ethical highway (**Lesson #2: Call Out Hypocrisy**).

Being alert to the mob mentality that forms around theories rather than facts is important for having a country that's based on truth and not fiction. We have to be ever-vigilant to the rise of fascism and the wolves in sheep's clothing who pretend to represent the country's interest but really are just representing their own. (**Lesson #3: Mixing with the Mob Is a Death Knell**).

It is important, going forward, that we keep our commitments—no more broken promises—and that we have the courage and toughness to solve the problems we have now and those that lie ahead, on very local levels but also more nationally and globally. (**Lesson #4: Strive to Learn Toughness through Adversity; Lesson 5: Keep Your Commitments;** and **Lesson 6: Solve Problems for the Greater Good—The Place of Justice**). If we are to "right the ship," to reclaim the American Dream, we cannot cower in the face of power and might, whether economic, political, social, or military. Know that somewhere in this journey, we will all be asked to speak truth to power, as uncomfortable and frightening that may be. (**Lesson #10: Speak Truth to Power**). We have a prime example in Colonel Vinman, mentioned before, who testified before Congress against the Trump administration even though this imperiled his own career. And there have been many more. Speaking truth to power doesn't mean attacking and ransacking the Capitol, threatening the lives of people—that is a sure sign of cowardice. Rather, it means identifying the wrong that has been done, calling on evidence based on fact, not fiction.

Seeking the fulfillment of the American Dream for everyone in this country takes understanding our past, knowing where we come from, understanding that at one time or another our ancestors were considered "the other"—the undesirable, not intelligent enough or too disease-ridden to contribute anything to America. We need to see the human being, not the stereotype—to get past the labels and slogans, and come to know who lives beneath the skin. Knowing your truth, facing your fears of the unknown, of people who look different from you, who have different food or customs, and not letting that fear dictate your choices and behavior will inevitably open the door to a brighter, more engaging, and inclusive American Dream. (Lesson 7: See the Human in the Stereotype; Lesson 9: The "Other" Is You; and Lesson 11: Face Your Fears and Your Truth).

Finally, while I acknowledge that Alex wouldn't have recognized some of what I have written about him here, the lessons directly passed on by his actions and words speak volumes to me of how we live in this world today. "Patty Jo," he would say, "they [aristocrats] got here first; they set the rules." This always entices me to look beyond the structure and seek to understand why something is done or why a law is in place—what are its roots and who proscribed its frame-work. I also learned what doesn't work—being prejudiced based on skin color, gender, or some other superficial quality that is not based in fact but rather is grown from a myth that becomes a standard, that's only about keeping things the same for fear of opening the gates, and what that could mean in terms of one's own sense of well-being. The prejudice I saw played out locally is something I wouldn't want carried forward in any generation. I think about those Italian immigrants in 1900 in "Little Hell" whom the Scandinavians saw as ruining property values, or whom Henry Cabot Lodge felt were less intelligent. Can we *not* repeat this for the newest set of immigrants to touch these shores? Or for those still waiting to reap the benefits of the American prom-ise—African and Native Americans?

It is our solemn duty to move the promise of America forward so that those who came to these shores, whether free or enslaved,

Black Family in the 1950s

those already here, and those yet to come can all share in the promises made in the founding documents of the United States of America. This is important now more than ever, because we are at a watershed moment—not only for Americans but for all of us as global citizens. The American values codified in those documents, and formed by the tears and struggles of people throughout centuries, across continents and countries, are the antidote to tyranny, wherever it rears its head. The world I grew up in existed in other homes across the country—white, Black, brown, yellow, and red. My community wasn't more special or more significant than their communities; but because of skin color, education, jobs, etc., I had greater access to the possibilities. "Possible" must be a word for all. It's time to open the doors.

Laws don't always equal right

Call out hypocrisy

Beware of the mob mentality of fascism

Strive to learn toughness through adversity

Keep your commitments

Bring fairness to the problem

See the human in the stereotype

Love as the yeast for growth

Remember that the "other" was once you

Speak truth to power

Face your fears and your truth

To Continue the Conversation...

I have asked you in Chapter 10 to think about your own family's experiences and backgrounds and provide your thoughts about bridging the political and cultural divide we have currently and/or your ideas for reimagining the American Dream. I also mentioned having a "story board" to post ideas and see if there are patterns to our collective thinking, areas where we have commonality and synergy. My exact words were:

> Could we begin to build a storyboard across this country of inclusion, not exclusion? Of telling the truth, of getting facts right, of building bridges for assimilation, not barricades? Could we develop an American Dream website where your ideas can potentially have a wider audience, with posting of real results from conversations and communal action?

To fulfill this intention, I am (as mentioned earlier) providing an online place for these ideas to reside on the "We the People" page of my website: *www.patriciamarino.com*.

As a guide for your responses, your thinking, I would say that your ideas do not have to be full-blown. They could be just imaginative sparks as they come to you, or snippets of family history that have helped to frame your thoughts and approaches to life. Perhaps in remembering your own family history, your connection to the long ago, you may experience an "aha" moment where the information relates to perceptions of immigrants, or people who look different from that general European-accepted norm. You may have glimmerings, even full-fledged suggestions, for what we can do in our own communities to provide a welcome space . . . to create better understanding, .

. .to let our decisions *not* be made from fear but rather from fact and compassion.

If the contents of the past pages resonate with the readers of this book and there is a large response to it, then I will batch similar ideas, suggestions, and visions in order to capture their diversity, and put them on this website. So if you do not see your suggestion in its exact form, it may be that I have captured it in a different way while still holding the valuable contribution of your thoughts.

I suspect that we humans are more the same than different; and that while customs, mores, and backgrounds may differ, there is commonality about human hopes and dreams, whether one was raised in India or Indiana. This book was written to demonstrate that commonality, and to help us move beyond the categories, the boxes that humans often find themselves encased in, to "see the human below the skin"; to focus on what unites us rather than on what divides us.

I again invite you to visit my website, *www.patriciamarino.com*, therefore, and post your ideas, remembrances, and connections to long ago. Just click the tab "We the People" and enter your reflections from there.

I hope you have enjoyed this journey as much as I have enjoyed creating the path. My hope is that the road forward is one of accountability, healing, and creating a better future for all in this community of Americans. It is my hope that the great experiment of democracy is transitioning to one that truly realizes the promise of the vision created back in the 18th century and that—with your help—gets to come into flower in our time.

Endnotes

Introduction

[1] "The American Dream." Merriam-Webster Dictionary. https://www.merriam-webster.com/

[2] "What Is the American Dream?" https://www.thebalance.com/

Chapter 2: The Reckoning

[3] https://www.britannica.com/topic/Magna-Carta

[4] https://www.history.com/topics/black-history/black-codes#

[5] https://www.history.com/topics/american-civil-war/reconstruction

[6] https://www.history.com/topics/early-20th-century-us/jim-crow-laws

Chapter 3: The Setting of the Joy: Lessons from the Alexander Francis School of Life

[7] https://www.britannica.com/event/Prohibition-United-States-history-1920-1933

[8] "Frank Sinatra: All or Nothing at All," Netflix 2015

[9] https://www.history.com/

[10] https://www.chicagomag.com/arts-culture/August-2017/The-South-Sides-Last-Remaining-Jazz-Landmarks/

[11] https://www.worldhistoryedu.com/lyndon-b-johnson-accomplishments/

[12] https://www.myjournalcourier.com/news/article/Illinois-political-scandals-are-nothing-new-12640525.php

[13] http://www.mikefelten.com/id10.html

[14] *Chicago Tribune*, March 20, 1940

Chapter 4: 902 Cambridge Avenue—The Old Neighborhood

[15] "Always," Irving Berlin, 1925.

[16] Dance Halls. https://www.chicagohistory.org/

[17] "And They Came to Chicago" (documentary), http://www.italiansofchicago.com/

[18] https://history.state.gov/milestones/1921-1936

[19] Dominic Candeloro, "Chicago's Italians: Immigrants, Ethnics, Achievers 1850-1985," https://www.lib.niu.edu/1999/iht629936.html

[20] Rudolph J. Vecoli, "The formation of Chicago's 'Little Italies,'" *Journal of American Ethnic History*, Vol. 2, No. 2 (Spring, 1983), pp. 5-20. Published by University of Illinois Press on behalf of the Immigration & Ethnic History Society, https://www.jstor.org/stable/27500267 (downloaded from 108.91.27.160 on 12 October 2019).

21 Dominic Candeloro, "Rundown of Chicago Italian Neighborhoods and churches: There was never, just ONE Little Italy in Chicago," September 18, 2013, http://libblogs.luc.edu

22 Candeloro, "Little Sicily, St. Philip Benizi Parish, Fr. Luigi Giambastiani, Chicago Catholic Immigrants Conference," November 5, 2013, http//:libblogs.luc.educ/ccic/little-sicily

23 Ibid.

24 Calogero Lombardo, "A Brief History of Chicago's Little Sicily Neighborhood and the Saint Philip Benizi Parish." Posted by Dominic Candeloro, Chicago Immigrants Conference, November 5, 2013, http://libblogs.luc.edu/ccic/little-sicily-st-philip-benizi-parish-fr-luigi-giambastiani/

25 John Bodnar, "Mutual Benefit Societies," *Chicago History,* 2005, http://www.encyclopedia.chicagohistory.org/pages/866.html

26 *Chicago Police Digest,* April 1940.

27 https://www.history.com/topics/world-war-ii/battle-of-the-bulge

Chapter 5: The Part of Our Part

28 "Who Gets Food Stamps? White People, Mostly," in *Huffington Post.* https://www.huffpost.com/entry/food-stamp-demographics_n_6771938#:~:text=According%20to%202013%20data%20from,1.2%20percent%20are%20Native%20American

29 Chinese Exclusion Act—1882, Definition & Purpose https://www.history.com/topics/immigration/chinese-exclusion-act-1882#:~:text=Meant%20to%20curb%20the%20influx,law%20on%20May%206%2C%201882

30 Ibid.

31 "A Brief History of America's Hostility to a Previous Generation of Mediterranean Migrants—Italians," https://theworld.org/stories/2015-11-26/brief-history-america-s-hostility-previous-generation-mediterranean-migrants

32 Soo Youn, "How Russia Used Facebook to Expand the Kremlin's Messaging," ABC News, January 17, 2019, https://abcnews.go.com/Business/russia-facebook-expand-kremlins-messaging/story?id=60445181#

Chapter 6: Pragmatism and Power Structures

33 Ann Morrell, "Whatever Happened to Trading Stamps?" July 31, 2015, https://www.democratandchronicle.com/story/news/local/roc-roots/2015/07/31/whatever-happened-trading-stamps/30963275/

Chapter 7: My Suffering, My Rights, My Governance

[34] Brian Mattmiller, "Study debunks myth that early immigrants quickly learned English," October 16, 2008, https://news.wisc.edu/study-debunks-myth-that-early-immigrants-quickly-learned-english/

[35] Esther Fleming, "What was the earliest settlement in America?" April 4, 2020, SidmartinBio, https://www.sidmartinbio.org/

[36] America's Untold Story," PBS International, https://pbsinternational.org/programs/Americas-untold-story/

Chapter 8: The Sacred Trust—Promises Unfulfilled

[37] A.V. Margavio and Jerome J. Salomone, *Bread & Respect: The Italians of Louisiana*. New Orleans: Pelican, 2014.

[38] *Chicago Tribune,* February 14, 1875.

[39] *Inter Ocean,* May 8, 1900.

[40] Cabrini-Green housing development, Chicago, Illinois, United States, https://www.britannica.com/topic/Cabrini-Green

[41] Ibid.

[42] http://www.italiansofchicago.com/topics.html

[43] https://chicagoitalians.blogspot.com/

[44] "Citizens Fight Housing Plan; Charge Deceit," *Chicago Tribune,* February 15, 1940.

[45] History of the Native Americans, https://indians.org/

[46] Joe McCarthy and Julie Ngalle, "The 5 Countries with the Most People Living in Slavery Today," May 22, 2017, https://www.globalcitizen.org./en/

[47] Banks, insurance companies limiting loans, mortgages, other services in specific geographic areas to prevent certain ethnicities from moving in.

[48] "Jumping the Broom," a history—African American Registry, https://aaregistry.org/

[49] Prof. Terra Hunter, "Slave Marriages, Families Were Often Shattered By Auction Block," NPR.

[50] https://www.history.com/

[51] Ibid.

[52] Pedro Bordalo, Katherine Coffman, Nicola Gennaioli, and Andrei Shleifer, "Stereotypes." First draft, November 2013/ this version, May 2015. https://scholar.harvard.edu/files/shleifer/files/stereotypes_june_6.pdf

[53] Dominic Candeloro, "Chicago's Italians: Immigrants, Ethnics, Achievers, 1850-1985" https://www.lib.niu.edu/1999/, p. 6.

54 "A Stark Reminder of How the US Forced American Indians into a New Way of Life," https://www.smithsonianmag.com/history/a-stark-reminder-of-how-the-us-forced-american-indians-into-a-new-way-of-life-3954109/

Chapter 9: Fragments to Fulfillment

55 J. R. Weil, *"Yellow Kid" Weil: The Autobiography of America's Master Swindler*. Spokane, WA: Nabat Books, 2011

56 Rex Martin, "The Concept of Rights," https://oxford.universitypressscholarship.com/view/10.1093/0198292937.001.0001/acprof-9780198292937-chapter-3

57 Nancy Flowers, "Human Rights Here and Now: Celebrating the Universal Declaration of Human Rights," *A Short History of Human Rights, http://hrlibrary.umn.edu/edumat/hreduseries/hereandnow/Part-1/short-history.htm*

58 Jane Johnson Lewis, "Madame de Stael Biography and Quotes," updated October 2017, *Madame de Stael Biography and Quotes, https://www.thoughtco.com/madame-de-stael-quotes-3530128*

59 "Income Inequality in the United States: Robert B. Reich Testimony before the Joint Economic Committee, United States Congress, January 16, 2014, https://www.jec.senate.gov/public/_cache/files/121e5a80-61e2-4c65-aa25-a06a1c0887d5/reich-testimony.pdf

60 "Fascism on the rise: where does it come from, and how to stop it, with a common European response," 30/10/2018, European Economic and Social Committee, https://www.eesc.europa.eu/

61 David Treuer, "Return the National Parks to the Tribes," *The Atlantic*, April 12, 2021.

62 *Forbes* 2020 Billionaire List.

63 "Does Capitalism Cause Poverty?" World Economic Forum, Ricardo Hausman, Founder-Director Growth Lab, Harvard University 2015.

64 Rachel Nuzum, "New Survey Data Shows Strong Support for Medicaid Expansion in States Most Likely to Determine 2020 Election Outcome," *The Commonwealth Fund*, October 29, 2020.

65 Daniel Burnham, Chicago architect (1864-1912).

66 "Native American Success Stories: Entrepreneurship Has Lifted Some Native Americans Out of Poverty," Foundation for Economic Education, https://fee.org/articles/native-american-success-stories/

67 Erin Blakemore, "How the GI Bill's Promise Was Denied to a Million Black WWII Veterans," https://www.history.com/news/gi-bill-black-wwii-veterans-benefits

[68] George M. Reynolds, "How Representative Is the All-Volunteer U.S. Military?" Council on Foreign Relations, April 15, 2018. https://www.cfr.org/

[69] Tim Lau, "Citizens United Explained," Brennan Center for Justice, December 12, 2019.

[70] Elizabeth Warren, "Getting the Big Money Out of Politics," 2022. http://elizabethwarren.com/plans/campaign-finance-reform

[71] "How Were the COVID-19 Vaccines Made So Fast?" *UC San Diego Health*, 1/1/21, L. Renee Watson, RN, Online Medical Reviewer

[72] Sara Holder and Kara Harris, "Where Calling the Police Isn't the Only Option," September 3, 2020, https://www.bloomberg.com/news/articles/2020-09-03/alternative-policing-models-emerge-in-u-s-cities

Chapter 10: Beloved Community

[73] James Baldwin and Margaret Mead. New York: Laurel Press, 1973.

[74] Laura Lynne Jackson, *Signs: The Secret Language of the Universe*, Part III, Navigating the Dark. New York: Dial Press, 2020.

[75] John Lewis, *Across That Bridge: A Vision for Change and the Future of America*. New York: Hachette Books, 2012.

Chapter 11: Lessons from America: Reflections on Adding Your Pieces to the American Mosaic

[76] 76. John G. Neihardt, *Black Elk Speaks* (Complete Edition). Lincoln, NB: Bison Books / University of Nebraska Press, p. 121 (Kindle Edition).

Photos & Illustrations

Photos are courtesy Patricia J. Marino collection, unless otherwise noted. Lesson graphics (on pgs. 41, 43, 47, 51, 56, 71, 75, 82, 93, 105, 140, and 192) are designed by Elena Karoumpali, L1graphics, https://99designs.com/ profiles/l1graphics.

Chapter 1: Remembering Fairfield Avenue

pg. 8, Mom and Dad (Ann Bublis Marino and Alexander Francis Marino)

pg. 9, Aunt Grace, Uncle Vito and Daughter, Honey

pg. 10, Lena and Frances

pg. 11, Justinian Society (125 Justinians in DC, 1960s) (Uncle Larry is in second row from back) *(Courtesy Dominic Candeloro, "Images of America,"* Italians in Chicago, *pp. 68-69)*

pg. 12, Young Uncle Larry

pg. 15, Aunt Rose

pg. 16, My mother in 1938

Chapter 2: The Reckoning

pg. 24, Black Codes *(www.slideshare.com)*

pg. 26, First United States Black Senator and US Representatives, 1872. "First Colored Senator and Representatives," Smithsonian National Portrait Gallery. (Hiram Rhoades Revels, 27 Sep 1827–16 Jan 1901; Benjamin Sterling Turner, 1825–1894; Josiah T. Walls, 1842–1905; Joseph Harvey Rainy, 1832–1887; R. Brown Elliot, 1842–1884; Robert Carlos De Large, 1842–14 Feb 1874; Jefferson Franklin Long, 3 Mar 1836–5 Feb 1900) *(Courtesy https://npg.si.edu/object/ npg_NPG.80.195)https://npg.si.edu/object/npg_NPG.80.195)*

Chapter 3: The Setting of the Joy: Lessons from the Alexander Francis School of Life

pg. 31, Alex and friends

pg. 33, The Guild Halloween Party—a fundraising group for our Parish (1960s)

Chapter 4: 902 Cambridge Avenue—The Old Neighborhood

pg. 58, Dad and Mom at one of their parties

pg. 59, The Old House—902 Cambridge Ave.

pg. 62, The Marino Clan (early 1950s)

pg. 63, Little Sicily, St. Philip Benizi Church *(Courtesy Dominic Candeloro,* Italians in Chicago, *p. 37)*

pg. 63, Sicilian Feast at St. Philip's *(Courtesy Dominic Candeloro,* Italians in Chicago, *p. 37)*

pg. 64, The Marinos at Paw Paw Lake, Michigan, 1941

pg. 73, Uncle Pete at the American Legion Hall (probably 1950s)

pg. 77, Aunt Mary, Aunt Lena, Dad, Grace, and Uncle Larry

pg. 78, Uncle Vito in the field contemplating planting

Chapter 5: The Part of Our Part

pg. 89, My family at a cousin's wedding in the 1950s, minus my brother Pete

Chapter 7: My Suffering, My Rights, My Governance

pg. 110, Uncle Vito enjoying a beer

Chapter 10: Beloved Community

pg. 170, Dad and Mom, July 1960

Epilogue: Lessons Learned in the Alexander Francis School of Life and Their Translation to a Re-Imagined American Dream

pg. 192, Black Family in the 1950s *(Courtesy https://www.bing.com/ images)*

Acknowledgments

Where does one begin? This memoir and reflection would not have seen the light of day unless I had been referred by a friend to Naomi Rose, whose name says it all; Naomi, from the Hebrew meaning "pleasant or gentle," and Rose, a name with many meanings, but compassion and confidentiality speak to me. I had no idea what I was writing or even if I could express what had been in my memory for a long time. When that expression hit the paper surface, it seemed confused and disconnected. Naomi's unbelievable patience and guidance through the process of write, edit, rewrite, edit was unwavering, but the gentle hand of Naomi guiding me helped me to stick to this project through my regular work, COVID, and through my doubts. She was the rudder of this ship to get me to the shore. Naomi then suggested I speak with her husband, Ralph Dranow, also an editor, who provided an amazing, intuitive, substantive critique of the writing, most of which I incorporated into this manuscript. These nuggets of comment helped to shape the work into a more understandable piece of writing. I remember his saying something like, "Pat, you know what this is about, and it's in your head, but you have to explain this to your audience." Thank you Ralph!

Along came Jane Majkiewicz, Write Intuition, who was a friend of Naomi's, a writer herself and editor, who began to critique the work structurally but ended up in a similar vein to Ralph, providing much more substantive comments to make the manuscript a more cogent, cohesive piece than its original version. Jane also edited my website content; and for both efforts, I am incredibly grateful.

A great big thank you to the *Readers* of this book who took the time to plow through the manuscript and offer advice and comment about what they drew from it, what spoke to them, what they didn't understand, what might be missing:

To my old and dear friend, Ann Curran, who I knew would be brutally honest with me, who I suspected would tell me to put down my pen. So I was totally surprised by the joy that leapt from her words about how much she loved the work. She said she took off her editing cap and got lost in the story.

To Dr. Glynda Hull, School of Education, University of California, Berkeley, for your critical eye and enthusiasm for both content and writing style.

My thanks to Dr. Dominic Candeloro, former Professor of History, University of Illinois and Loyola University Chicago, for responding to a perfect stranger, providing critique and reflection of the work, and photos from his own research and books on Italians in Chicago. I found my Uncle Larry's photo in his work, *Images of America: Italians in Chicago*.

To Brian Beverly, attorney, for his legal advice.

A great big thank you to my dear friend, Dr. Valerie Miles, DMin, Ph.D., Associate Professor, Ministerial Leadership & Practical Theology, American Baptist Seminary of the West—Graduate Theological Union, who I asked to review the manuscript for its perspective on African Americans' place in this country and the issue of forgiveness, as well as the overall worth of the work.

To my niece Justine, who reviewed a very early version of this manuscript and felt there were maybe three books in the copy, not one, thank you for your honesty. She made me rethink what I was writing. To Louie Gonzalez, an old friend who said about the first iteration of this book that he did not hear *my* voice; the work needed work! To Coach Tom Newell who kept telling me to trust my instincts and let the story unfold in its own way, thank you as well for believing I could actually do this. To Jacqui Diaz, a Boys & Girls Clubs of San Leandro colleague, for her thoughtful insights on clarity and her creative suggestions.

A special thank you to the "tactical team," as I will call them. To Gabriel Steinfeld of Steinfeld Proofreading, for his attention to detail. To Elena Karoumpali of L1graphics, for creating such a beautiful esthetic with both the book cover and the "lessons" visuals, which captured the soul of the book. And to Margaret Copeland of Terragrafix, book designer and typesetter, for pairing the interior design of the book with its focus.

Finally, and not the least, thank you to my children for their great gift of support to me. To Brian who said "Keep going"; to my dear, wonderful daughter, Alexis, for her support from the beginning, for being my cheerleader telling me I could do this, for taking a critical look at the various versions of the manuscript as it evolved, for never wavering in her love and caring.

To all of you—my enduring gratitude for taking this journey with me!

About the Author

Pat Marino began her career as a high school history/ESL teacher in Chicago and San Francisco, and her passion for history has always informed her perspective on her philanthropical endeavors, whether working with communities of color, or in education and youth development. She looks to history for guidance in understanding where we as a global community are in the growth of humanity, where we are headed, and what can we do differently to enable the next generation to improve the planet for all living beings.

Her current profession is as a philanthropic consultant, who brings more than 30 years of knowledge and experience in grantmaking and development to help funders and nonprofits achieve their charitable and organizational goals.

Pat worked for three Fortune 500 Oakland-based corporations in her career. She was president of The Clorox Company Foundation and co-chaired the East Bay Funders, a collaboration of 16 Bay Area foundations focused on neighborhood revitalization in Oakland and Richmond. In 2021, she completed a $10.5 million capital campaign for the Boys & Girls Clubs of San Leandro, California. These are all communities in the East Bay of California's San Francisco Bay Area. Pat brings a love of and background in education and youth development to her work.

Pat continues her work in philanthropy, helping expand the mission and growth of the Boys & Girls Clubs of San Leandro. She also continues to provide advice and counsel to other nonprofit organizations in the San Francisco Bay Area.

When not writing or consulting with nonprofit organizations, Pat loves to hike in the East Bay Regional Parks, hopes to resurrect her tennis game, and she enjoys traveling to the many places in California that make up its incredible natural and human diversity. In the coming years, she plans more travel in the U.S. and abroad, and looks forward to having more time to visit family and friends.

About Rose Press

Books to Bring You Home to Yourself
(A publishing house for your inner garden)
WWW.ROSEPRESS.COM

In our time of reading for information, Rose Press seeks to offer you books and other fragrant offerings that will live in your heart like an eternal time capsule, releasing their healing medicine as you need it.

"Fragrance" is not usually associated with books. Books, we tend to think, in our speeded-up age, are about ideas, entertainment, steps for helping us to be more new and improved.

And yet there have been books that are mirrors to the soul—or marvels of excavation, revealing the vast treasures hidden within. There have been books, the journey of whose reading swept readers up into their remarkable world, leaving them at the end with the passage of that journey in their bones, and the fragrance of that atmosphere still hovering invisibly near. There have been books so deeply entered into by their authors that turning the pages of these books transmitted to their readers more than a whiff of the understandings and evocations embodied in the book: they helped to form the readers' very being.

This is the vision of Rose Press books: that in taking them into yourself, you discover what is truly in you, and it opens your heart like petals opening to the light.

That said, getting to the more subtle fragrance—the distillation of more earthbound, sometimes sludgy experience—is often what book writers dream of and work in the trenches to do. Behind the most exquisite fragrance left with a reader by a book is the author's composted experience (all the years and memories and ideas and possibilities dreamed of and lived through, written and refined) that produced such perfume. So what is left on the page is the offering: the "fragrance," one might say. All the dregs have been churned up and left to sink to the bottom, leaving only the gift of the book.

This, then, is what the reader gets to experience: a hint of the churning process, but ultimately, the fragrance.

> *When 10,000 rose petals are gathered in the dark of early morning, placed into retorts filled with solvent, and heated over time until their oil rises as a liquid distillation, then you have just 16 ounces of that most prized (and expensive) of aromatics, rose essence (rose absolute).*
>
> *In the same way, Rose Press Books are the distillation of their authors' essence, distilled over time and many revisions to bring you into contact with the gift of something fragrant and indescribably beautiful within yourself.*

Writing these books entails a journey, and reading these books is also a journey. And you, afterwards, will be the carrier of that journey in the world: burnished, more yourself than before, and smelling—even after everything—like a rose.

CPSIA information can be obtained
at www.ICGtesting.com
Printed in the USA
JSHW041527270323
39505JS00002B/46

9 780981 627892